C000133329

Richard Smith's Guide To
GETTING EVEN!

▼▼▼

By Richard Smith

Workman Publishing
New York

To those who want to make their fantasies come true, especially when plagued by noisy neighbors, motorists who dawdle in the passing lane, arrogant bureaucrats, surly salesclerks, callers who put you on hold and, perhaps most life-threatening, co-workers with baby photos.

Text copyright © 1994 by Richard Smith

Library of Congress Cataloging-in-Publication Data
Smith, Richard.
[Guide to getting even]
Richard Smith's Guide to getting even : 143 lessons in etiquette for a world gone mad / by Richard Smith.
p.   cm.
ISBN 0-89480-478-2 (pbk.)
1. Etiquette—Humor.   I. Title.   II. Title: Guide to getting even.
PN6231.E8S63   1993
818'.5402—dc20   93-14448
                                                              CIP

Workman books and calendars are available at special discounts when purchased in bulk for premiums and sales promotions as well as for fund-raising or educational use. Special editions can also be created to specification. For details, contact the Special Sales Director at the address below.

Workman Publishing Company, Inc.
708 Broadway
New York, NY 10003

Manufactured in the United States of America

10   9   8   7   6   5   4   3   2   1

Contents

▼▼▼

OCCUPATIONAL HAZARDS

DON'T TREAD ON ME

FED UP

FUTILE ATTRACTIONS

VIEWER DISCRETION

Introduction

▼▼▼

How to deal with problem people—pests who make us wish we could walk around carrying a concealed weapon, like our very own Polaris missile? The owner who thinks it's cute when his dog uses your leg to achieve Spaniel Ecstasy. The person who barges ahead of you on line. The motorist behind you who honks the instant the light changes. And, of course, on the bus, the little old (but robust) lady who thinks she deserves your seat and tries to make you feel guilty. (Be polite: offer to hold her cane steady.)

My personal enlightenment began on a checkout line at the supermarket as I stood there, impatiently waiting while the cashier tried to count out my change and carry on a conversation with a co-worker simultaneously. Doesn't the customer come first? I thought as I glanced outside, wondering who'd reach my illegally-parked-in-a-handicapped-space car first: me or the officer with the summons book. Ordinarily a courteous person, I suddenly found myself shouting, "PLEASE, MISS, I NEED MY CHANGE BEFORE CHRISTMAS," then watched in amazement as she clamped her mouth shut and quickly finished putting money into my hand.

Finally, instead of suffering in polite silence, I'd done what I really felt like doing, and it worked! But would it work again? The next day at the bank, when I tried to make a withdrawal, I was told by an insufficiently apologetic teller, "Our computers are down." Instead of timidly walking away, I placed my head on the counter, closed my eyes and told the teller to wake me up when the computers were up. Maybe my snoring was too loud, perhaps it was the throw pillow I carry for such occasions, but suddenly I was permitted to make a withdrawal!

That night at an expensive restaurant, I again tested my new etiquette system. When shown to our table, I decided that two full-size adults should not have to pay for food eaten on a surface barely larger than a dinner check. (The maître d' refused to give us a larger table, even though I swore we'd eat enough for four). "We'll be back when we shrink," I explained and walked out, content to dine in comfort in an enormous booth at Denny's.

This, then, is an etiquette manual suggesting what one half of America would like to do to the other half were it legal—a guide for the person fed up with doing the "right" thing . . . and suffering the consequences. There was the lady, for instance, who wrote and asked me how to get rid of persistent insurance salesmen. (Use behavior modification: brandish a cattle prod.) A troubled city dweller wondered if there was a tactful solution to the proliferation of panhandlers in her neighborhood. (Parachuting them into the woods with a bag of seed, a mule and a good-luck handshake is one alternative.) And an executive who believes time is money asked how to cope with an associate who speaks too slowly. (Reach out and move his tongue faster.)

Although many questions did not pertain strictly to etiquette, I felt their subject matter justified a reply. "What," asked one young man, "is the appropriate response when my boss makes a welcome sexual advance?" (Demand a raise.) I can't tell you how many moviegoers wondered whether there wasn't a way, other than ether, to silence certain mammals who talk while the film is in progress. And one frustrated social security applicant, referring to her treatment by an arrogant but bottom-of-the-gene-pool government official, asked about the propriety of inflicting bodily harm. (Yes, but don't say Mr. Smith suggested it.)

As an etiquette counselor, I am gratified that readers are already reporting success at everything from refusing to look at wedding photos to feeling newly empowered when the plumber fails to show. I caution, however, against going too far. One correspondent, in a fit of rage, took the law into her own hands against a restaurant reviewer who revealed the name of her favorite undiscovered restaurant. (She was let off with just a warning—the judge ate there, too.)

NOTE: In reading my answers one might wonder, "These solutions, Mr. Smith, are they lawful?" Happily, in most cases, the answer is perhaps.

Invasions
of Privacy

▼▼▼

Who are these people who, uninvited, think they have a right to invade our personal space? I'm talking not only about aggressive car salesmen who insist on shaking your hand (forcing you to spend the rest of the day trying to wash Aramis off your palm) and "activists" who wave Save the Earthworm petitions in your face and tell you how to live your life, but the full range of pests: relatives who "happen" to drop by at dinner time (have them relax in the garage until you've finished eating); grown children who won't leave home, then get annoyed when you change the locks; total strangers who, without permission, show photos of their pet; and people on post office lines who just stand there when the clerk calls "Next!" (yield to that irresistible impulse—place your hands on their shoulders and propel them forward).

You can't hide. These people are everywhere. Several letters mentioned unwelcome surprise visitors such as Jehovah's Witnesses and Bible salesmen who won't be deterred (sit them down and tell them about your gallbladder operation—don't forget to show them the scar), as well as people who monopolize cash machines (speed things up by leaning over, staring at the screen and asking, "Gee, is that all the money you have?"). And one upset party hostess in Indiana, Pennsylvania, wondered whether putting uninvited guests to work washing glasses was polite (yes, and send them out for more liquor).

This section, then, is dedicated to those decent, overconsiderate people who haven't yet learned to say a) "No," b) Sorry, I don't have the time, or c) "The party's over."

Neigh-Boors

Dear Mr. Smith:

The people who live above me walk around in heavy shoes, play loud music late at night and encourage their overweight son to bounce around on a pogo stick. Courteous phone calls and polite notes have been useless. Twice I knocked on their door, but they couldn't hear me because of the noise. When I sent them a tape of me howling in pain, I got it back with a note saying, "You sing nice." I haven't had a decent night's sleep since last May. What can I do so I a) remain a good neighbor and b) don't go to jail?

—Sleepy

Dear Sleepy:

Thousands of thoughtful, mild-mannered people, because they live beneath savages, face a nightly moral dilemma: polite phone call or baseball bat? Two solutions:

Good—Move. Not out of the building, but to an apartment directly above your noisy neighbors. Exercise nightly by dribbling a bowling ball or (author's choice) practicing standing broad jumps.

Best—Affix speakers to your ceiling. Insert a repeating CD of either "The Stars and Stripes Forever" or "The Best of the Mormon Tabernacle Choir" and set the control at full volume. Go away for the summer.

"Last Call"

Dear Mr. Smith:

When I have a party at my house, how do I deal with guests who can't take a hint that the evening is finally over? No matter how late it's getting, no matter how extravagant my yawns, they simply will not leave, even though I'm standing there in my bathrobe, flicking the lights on and off and yelling, "Take your drinks with you!"

—Nodding Off

Dear Nodding:

Your parties are too successful. When all else fails (hiring a butler with body odor, training your sheepdog to herd unwanted guests into the front hall):

1. Open the front door.
2. Run around to the back of the house.
3. Get a firm grip on the foundation.
4. Slowly tilt the house forward.
5. Watch remaining guests slide into the street.

———

CONFIDENTIAL TO "TIPPER" IN WASHINGTON: It's effective, but I caution against hastening the departure of late-staying guests by spraying them with your garden hose.

"Don't Call Us"

Dear Mr. Smith:

What do I do about a next-door neighbor who habitually drops by for coffee without calling first? Her visits cut into my TV programs, and she never knows when to leave. This morning, when I answered the door naked with a toothbrush hanging from my mouth, she asked, "Is this a bad time?"

—Reluctant Hostess

Dear Reluctant:

When she knocks again, wave to her through the door window, smile and resume what you're doing. If she doesn't go away, open the door, ask her how she takes her coffee, hand her a steaming mug plus a cruller, remind her to return the mug when she's finished, point her south and firmly escort her off your property.

CONFIDENTIAL TO L.S. IN SCARSDALE: Wouldn't it be nice if, in addition to burglar alarms, our homes were equipped with an early warning alert system (Watch It! Unidentified Neighbor Approaching!) that automatically closed the drapes, doused the house lights and hid your car in the garage?

Neither a Borrower . . .

Dear Mr. Smith:

Why aren't people more responsible? When a friend asked to borrow $100 "just until payday," I didn't have the nerve to say no. That was two months ago. Now I need the money, but it would make me uncomfortable to ask her for it. I need billing assistance.

—Lone Shark

Dear Lone:

Call this former friend and ask to borrow $100 "just until payday." She'll get the hint.* There's nothing worse than having to remind borrowers to pay you back, especially if they assume one of those "Hey, you'll get your money" attitudes. I used to practice a visualization technique in which I pictured my money being returned to me. Alas, it never worked. Now, when asked for money, I tell the applicant, "Sorry, I'm an etiquette counselor, not a banker."

---

* If she says she doesn't have it, do what the big collection agencies do. Either call 40 times a day or, to save message units, send a collector with a low hairline named Vito. (No, you may not pawn her dog.)

None of Your Business

Dear Mr. Smith:

Why can't people take no for an answer? Everyone keeps asking for my recipes (I'm a great cook), but I really hate to give them out. Many are my own creations, some are family heirlooms and several I've already shredded. I feel bad, however, when I have to refuse. Can you help?

—Secretive

Dear Secretive:

Haven't these people heard of cookbooks? Or privacy? Cure them of their curiosity by revealing your recipes, but include strange ingredients. To your baked Alaska, for instance, add Kraft Singles, and make sure that chocolate sprinkles are listed when you hand over your "for your eyes only" recipe for lobster bisque (with a psychotic aside like "To be eaten on organic melba toast"). I don't think they'll want more recipes.*

NOTE: I freely give out my secret recipe for Atomic Meat Loaf. It gives me an excuse to visit friends in the hospital.

---

* If they do, you've tapped into a new market. Obtain a small business loan and open a neighborhood restaurant immediately.

H AVING BEEN ASSAULTED, at various times in my life, by 1) a child playing "The Beer Barrel Polka" on the accordion; 2) a friend's wife, after only 200 voice lessons, singing the entire score from *Aida* (at least they offered to pay for my convalescence) and 3) an amateur magician, I have to ask, why don't people know they're supposed to remain seated?

Grossland

Dear Mr. Smith:

Is there anything scarier than a performing child? At a recent gathering, the host's six-year-old son, without warning, suddenly got up and, strumming a broom, did an Elvis impersonation—and his parents didn't stop him! The martini and three white wines I'd already had did little to numb my senses—I had to sit there smiling politely through "Hound Dog," "Jail House Rock" and, as an encore, a tribute to Carl Perkins. Not only was the kid off-key and uncoordinated, but afterwards neither he nor his parents apologized.

—Still in Shock

Dear Shocked:

How can any sensitive person not panic when, at a party, a child picks up even a real musical instrument and starts making singing motions? You were clearly a victim of guest abuse. Before such an event, a decent, caring host would have given each guest a painkiller, like Tylenol, or a $100 bill. (*Note:* Revenge is sweet—get back at the host by pilfering valuable knickknacks. Get back at the child by either stepping on his foot or smiling and whispering in his ear, "Did you know you're illegitimate?")

———

CONFIDENTIAL TO GRANDMA IN TALLAHASSEE: Don't worry about the mental effect of having to watch your untalented granddaughter tap-dance whenever you visit. It only affects those parts of the brain used to watch Cher demonstrate hair-care products.

Post-Dramatic Stress Syndrome

Dear Mr. Smith:

At my brother-in-law's wedding, I had to listen to someone who didn't drink enough sing "Feelings." It happened so suddenly, I didn't have time to refresh my own drink. Where is these people's sense of shame?

—Stunned

Dear Stunned:

I can't help it. When this happens to me, I always laugh until white wine runs out of my nostrils. People like that have a pathological need to be targets of a) attention and b) tomatoes. Research shows that sitting through an amateur performance of anything can be more life-threatening even than watching a Miss Teen Beauty Pageant. Next time you're trapped, pass the time by:

1. Tossing pennies at the performer.

2. Throwing a tablecloth over the performer and dragging him back to his chair—you'll be praised for heroism.

3. Studying your table's centerpiece to see if it's worth stealing.

4. Leaving.

Party Animal

Dear Mr. Smith:

How does a civilized person deal with a mime? After buttonholing me at a party, one proceeded to act out what appeared to be either a dying swan or a mental patient eating porridge. What does one do with these people? Tip them? Offer them counseling? This one finally went away when I acknowledged his presence (by smoothing clam dip on his face), but that didn't stop him permanently—he went on to annoy several other guests.

—Struck Dumb

Dear Dumb:

There are many odious forms of entertainment—charades, organ grinders, vacation slides and, of course, baton twirling. I've always felt, however, that mimes deserve special punishment, especially those whose act includes a hand puppet. Fortunately, there are courteous ways to deal with these nuisances. One friend of mine carries insect repellent; another uses a riding crop. The best solution I've heard came from a woman in New Orleans, who demands encores till the mime goes insane and starts speaking in tongues.

Emergency Room

Dear Mr. Smith:

I think people, especially wives, who monopolize the bathroom are rude, particularly those who a) ignore my persistent knocking and b) mumble something unprintable when I ask, "Are you ever coming out of there?" The worst offenders are those who enter the bathroom with a copy of Reader's Digest *and refuse to emerge until they've finished "It Pays to Increase Your Word Power." How do I get them to budge?*

—*Squirming*

Dear Squirming:

Use the time to compose several love notes, to be slipped under the door one by one:

▲ *Urgent*—"Are you ever coming out of there?"
▲ *More urgent*—"Other people are waiting."
▲ *Loving*—"I miss you."
▲ *More loving*—"The children miss you."
▲ *Health-conscious*—"At least open a window."

NOTE: Is there a causal connection between reading on the toilet and the boom in Preparation H sales? Only the FDA knows for sure. I do worry when I enter a bathroom and see a stack of literature. Has it been touched before or after the reader has washed his hands?

LIKE MUSIC IN STORES and public buildings, those artificial scents that haunt so many cars and houses are practically impossible to escape. Trust me—despite what the ads say, in no way are these manufactured odors like "letting the outdoors inside" (unless, of course, you live next to a hazardous waste site). In cars, the culprit's usually a cardboard "pine tree" that smells suspiciously like industrial cleanser. In homes, I've breathed everything from potpourri to a sachet bag containing a carefully formulated mixture of Airwick and Wet Dog. (And there's always that can of Glade on the bathroom windowsill, which, before Enlightenment, I assumed was to relieve constipation.) What are people trying to hide?

Cover-Up

Dear Mr. Smith:

My boyfriend bought a pine-scented air freshener for his car. Not only does it look stupid dangling from the rear-view mirror, but it makes the car smell like a gypsy cab. If I ride with my head out the window, my rollers blow off. Can you help?

—Can't Breathe

Dear Breathless:

In a perfect world, drivers like your boyfriend, when stopped by police, would get three points on their license—one for driving under the influence, two for waging chemical warfare. If your boyfriend's not too bright, tell him car fresheners cause impotence (they do). If he's thrifty, explain that their weight consumes extra fuel. Unfortunately, there are only two known antidotes to car freshener: 1) riding in the trunk and 2) gas fumes.

You-Reeka!

Dear Mr. Smith:

Can something be done about the growing national problem of room fresheners? When visiting friends, instead of being greeted by a homey aroma (baking bread or simmering marinara would be nice), we are affronted by chemical smells that supposedly resemble a "floral whisper" or "summer breeze" but actually remind us of why we left New Jersey. Should we tell them that an honest smell, like garlic frying in olive oil or a baby that needs changing, is preferable to perfume potpourri or honeysuckle plug-ins?

—Fresh-Air Fiends

Dear Fiends:

You could ask to be seated by an open window, especially if there's a draft. Maybe they'll get the hint. People with taste know that fresheners may be used only in emergencies—to cover up the smell of:
1. A fried calamari experiment gone awry
2. Three-week-old kitty litter
3. A bathroom whose:
    a. Ventilator is malfunctioning
    b. Window is painted shut
4. Grandpa

Greetings!

Dear Mr. Smith:

Help! Every Christmas we receive several "yearly roundup" letters from distant acquaintances informing us about their families and how they spent the past year. Not only are these people dull, but they have the nerve to include detailed information about their pets— "In September, Skippy experienced heartburn but we changed his birdseed brand . . . we were so worried." To make matters worse, they enclose a family photo (these are not, I assure you, great-looking families). Is there a polite way to get off their mailing lists?
—Prefer Mail from Publisher's Clearing House

Dear Prefer:

Previously, when two or three of these letters would come in the mail, I'd write "Deceased" and "Return to Sender" on the envelope. Now, however, I find that after four glasses of eggnog these mini-bios become hysterically funny. I even take a pen and fill the margins with helpful notes: "Maybe it's better that Frank lost his job. Now he can find himself." . . . "Sorry about Myra's mood swings. Have you considered going a bit easier on the fast food?" . . . "That third child on the left, is it a girl or a boy?" I then return the letters to each appreciative family. (Good news: their letters have begun to taper off.)

Mother-in-Law Non Grata

Dear Mr. Smith:

My mother-in-law has a home of her own, but she doesn't have a life of her own. She's constantly at our house, fussing, telling me how to raise my kids, what to cook, how to clean and, when she thinks I'm out of earshot, asking her son why he married me in the first place. Please help—I'm about to snap.

—At Wits' End

Dear At Wits':

In-laws are for baby-sitting and leaving you money, not for telling you how to run your life. The next time your mother-in-law sits down on your sofa, have it covered with vinyl. You'll be able to see her; she'll be able to see you, but you won't be able to hear a word she says. (*Note:* So she doesn't feel rejected, wave to her from time to time.)

ALTERNATE OPTION

Consider building a nap-activated In-Law Porch. After dinner, while they're sitting there, dozing on the swing, the porch detaches from the house, slowly rolls away and doesn't stop until it reaches Toronto.

A LAS, A MOTHER'S LOVE doesn't stop when you leave home or when you finally hang up the phone after she calls for the third time that week to find out if you're wearing your muffler. She is always busy loving you. Several correspondents complained of mailboxes constantly stuffed with care packages—cartons of high-fat homemade cookies and socks you wouldn't wear on a bet. One daughter mentioned receiving, over the past three years, 2,500 grapefruits from her mother in Florida. The most dangerous mothers, however, are those with knitting needles.

Clothes Horse

Dear Mr. Smith:

I love my mother, but she sends me clothing that she knits herself. To wear her sweaters I have to contort my body, and everyone says I look like Quasimodo. Is there a tactful way to ask her for heirlooms, or money, instead?

—Mama's Boy

Dear Mama's Boy:

Is it possible we have the same mother? My solution: as soon as I open the parcel, I have a photograph taken of a smiling me wearing the sweater. Then I send the picture to Mom and the sweater to the attic. Someday I'll open a boutique.

It's the Gift That Counts, Not the Thought

Dear Mr. Smith:

Is there a way to get back at people who give you dreadful gifts? For our wedding someone gave us a vase that obviously came from a hospital gift shop, and at our housewarming an aunt gave us a porcelain rooster that she actually assumes will be displayed in our new home.* Don't these people realize a) we embarrass easily and b) such gifts lower property values?

—Want to Buy a Doily?

Dear Unfortunate:

First, never send thank-you notes to people afflicted with a taste disorder—it just encourages them. Some choices:

1. If the gift is fragile, a) place it on the very edge of a table, then b) bang into the table and c) watch it smash on the floor. (Don't forget to say "Oops.")

2. Put the item in your driveway. Someone's sure to drive over it.

3. Repaint it and give it back to them for Christmas.

4. Donate it to charity and chance a questionable tax deduction.

---

* Would that it were able to cluck and fly away.

CONFIDENTIAL TO J.N. IN PHOENIX RE DISPOSITION OF A CANDY DISH THAT EVEN YOUR DOG REFUSES TO EAT FROM: Either 1) trash it or 2) pray it isn't dishwasher-safe.

THE PASS-ALONG PROBLEM

▼▼▼

In addition to weapons and drugs, let's ban other dangerous substances like gifts that make the recipients wonder a) "What did I do to deserve this," b) "How do I conceal my disappointment?" and c) "What do I do with it?" Many such items are what experts refer to as "pass-alongs," repulsive tchachkes once given to the donor who, being cheap, regives them to you in the guise of a thoughtful present. Preowned gifts are easily spotted, however. Beware of:

▲ Candy dishes and figurines. (No exceptions.)

▲ A tie or scarf that's been carefully ironed.

▲ Yogurt makers and other eerie kitchen appliances.

▲ Any item that doesn't quite fit the box it comes in.*

▲ A book that looks new but has a telltale tea stain on page 117.

▲ Any fruitcake with an expiration date.

* Jewelry that comes in a Tiffany box but looks like it was purchased from a street vendor is particularly suspect.

Phonees

Dear Mr. Smith:

I'm in a restaurant, trying to enjoy a meal, and the person at the next table is using (or should I say shouting into) a cellular phone. He thinks he's so cool, but a) he looks silly and b) his conversation is boring beyond belief. Am I overreacting?

—Indignant

Dear Indignant:

No. Cellular phones in cars or buses are bad enough, but at a restaurant table? I'd take a swing at him (unless he's making an urgent call to the Board of Health—"Hello, I'm having dinner at Rocco's Trattoria and I just discovered rodent droppings in my pasta"). You have every right to lean over and ask, "Is this conversation necessary? The microwaves are curdling my gazpacho."

A cellular phone should be used only:

1. If it's concealed in a brown paper bag.

2. If the subject matter is appropriate (such as calling a "psychic friend" to find out where you parked your car).

3. In a restaurant, to call the chef to ask what he puts in his fabulous veal marsala.

4. In a car, when approaching a toll plaza, to alert the toll collector that you don't have exact change.

Assault with a Deadly Weapon

Dear Mr. Smith:

What can you say to people who smoke where they're not supposed to? I'm bothered by tobacco fumes, but I'm also easily intimidated—especially if the smoker looks mean.

—Gasp

Dear Gasp:

Polite words have no effect on these people—they're too busy coughing. A true anti-smoking zealot carries scissors and, without uttering a word, snips off the glowing tip of the cigarette, then runs for his life.

THE POUND OF MUSIC

▼▼▼

So many letters complaining about loud car stereos. People with delicate ears wondering how to cope with pain caused by 10 blaring speakers in a car driven by one mental defective. No one, of course, has a right to make the world listen to his music, whether it comes from a car or a boom box. (And it's always such dreadful music. Why is it never Bach, or Mozart, or Billie Holiday?) One correspondent pulls alongside the offending car and gets sick all over its door. His wife, a security guard, opting for something less melodramatic, shoots paint balls at the windshield. Another correspondent, a promising minor league pitcher, fires eggs through the open window and, after observing the yoke sliding down the driver's face, speeds off to batting practice. And my personal etiquette consultant, a golfer, marvels at how efficiently a boom box is rendered silent with a six-iron.

Alarmist

Dear Mr. Smith:

How do I get back at someone whose wailing car alarm keeps me up all night? Tactful notes on the windshield haven't helped, calling the police is useless and I can't afford a motel.

—Groggy

Dear Groggy:

A universal problem that's getting worse. It wouldn't be so bad if you heard the alarm because the car was actually being stolen (at least the thief would drive it out of the neighborhood and you'd finally get some sleep). The answer, of course, is reprisal. If, at 1 A.M., a car alarm goes off, take a stool, park yourself beside the offending vehicle (carefully, you don't want Simoniz on your pajamas) and let the air out of the tires. If the owner doesn't take the hint and the alarm goes off the next night, compose a polite note like "Love your siren" and either:

1. Nail it to his windshield;* or
2. Etch it (in italics) on the glass.

---

* If you don't have a nail, use a high-gloss enamel to paint your sentiment on the offender's windshield.

PET PEEVES

▼▼▼

As a confirmed animal lover (especially of those not already in captivity), responding to the complaints in this section was painful since it's usually the indulgent owner rather than his or her pet who needs obedience training.

A playful Akita with muddy paws doesn't know not to welcome a guest by jumping up on her new silk pants. (*Note:* When the owner says doggie's just being playful, smile and respond, "Me too," as you wipe your chocolate-covered hands on the dog owner's new cashmere sweater.) To a dog, all the world's a men's room—he doesn't know that even the heartiest lawn is no match for 200 pounds of poo. (If I time it right, I can turn on my lawn sprinkler and watch as my neighbor's toy terrier, while doing his business, flies six feet into the air.) And the dog who barks all night doesn't realize he's devaluing the neighborhood. Why aren't pet owners as kind to people as they are to their animals?*

---

* I've always wondered how even the most loving owner, when walking his dog, can bend over, newspaper in (or baggie over) one hand, and gingerly pick up his animal's warm deposit. Would he do the same for his wife?

Hot Dogs

Dear Mr. Smith:

How do I discourage my friends' collie from sniffing my crotch? They think it's cute and tell me, "He likes you," but I'm sensitve in that area and he has a snout like a bayonet.

—Ticklish

Dear Ticklish:

Too many owners assume that everyone treasures their pet—yet never once have I been reimbursed, at the end of the evening, for the Alpo stains on my Ralph Laurens. You could, of course, protect yourself by inserting the dog's nose in a vase as soon as you arrive,* but that might threaten your friendship. Instead, bring an enormous steak bone and watch doggie spend the evening trying to bury it in the rug.

* Will not work on a bulldog. Use a bucket.

CONFIDENTIAL TO K.P. IN ST. LOUIS: You *should* be outraged when your neighbor's dachshund wanders over and befouls your prized peonies. Returning the dog by drop-kicking it over your hedge is, however, cruel. Use UPS instead.

Just "Doo" It

Dear Mr. Smith:

The other day when, for the tenth time that week, my neighbor allowed his dog to "poop" in my driveway, mild-mannered me got testy. I called my neighbor over and in a friendly manner pressed his nose into the dog's steaming mound. At the same time, I hit him gently on the head with a rolled-up newspaper and repeated, "Naughty owner, mustn't let his dog do that." I thought this would be good training. Did I "doo" the correct thing?

—Samaritan

Dear Samaritan:

I'm an opponent of vigilantism, but in this case—bravo! I got several letters on this very subject, but I published yours because it contains by far the most direct and least controversial solution. The other writers were, frankly, too genteel: one merely used a slingshot to return the dog's droppings to the offending owner; another actually went through the legal system, placing the dog's deposit in a box and then having the animal hauled into court for trespassing.

THE PROPER THING

You may also step in the dog's deposit, then visit the owner at his home and walk on the carpets. (Especially effective on pastel Orientals.)

At Your Disservice

▼▼▼

Is the customer always right? Not according to my mail. There were stacks of letters from irate shoppers, all victimized by the very people they were giving their money (and employment) to—insolent cashiers, dysfunctional salesclerks and indifferent managers. (Frequent customer grievances: being scolded for daring to interrupt a store employee who was thumbing through *The Star* or asking, "Do you have this in my size?" and being told, "How should I know?")

Churlish employees are not the only problem. Customers themselves can be inconsiderate, keeping those behind them standing an extra 20 minutes in a register line because they insist on paying by personal check (which, of course, the manager, who is dozing in the meat locker, has to approve) or suddenly remember an item they forgot and disappear into the farthest reaches of the store while everyone waits.

Unfortunately, due to space limitations, I could respond only to a few letters and hope that those of you whose questions remain unanswered ("How hard may I squeeze the fruit without incurring the wrath of the manager?" or "How do I deal with the scathing glance of a store owner when I walk out without buying anything?") will not be disappointed. I must, however, advise "Cheated in Philadelphia" that being overcharged by a checkout scanner is a reverse form of shoplifting—the store is stealing from the customer! (Why is the error never in the shopper's favor?) I strongly suggest charging the store manager with theft and placing him under citizen's arrest.

Can't They Count?

Dear Mr. Smith:

What do I do when I'm on the "10 Items or Less" line and the woman ahead of me has 17 items in her cart, completely ignoring the sign?

—Ever Vigilant

Dear Vigilant:

Instead of saying something, which might cause bad feelings, simply take the additional items out of the offender's cart and place them on the floor.

ETIQUETTE ADVISORY

You're thrilled to see just one shopper ahead of you in the checkout line. In moments you'll be out of the store (you think). Then, as you begin to empty your cart, the cashier announces, "I'm closed." What should you do? Slink away to another register and stand behind 19 people, each with an overflowing grocery cart? Never. Instead, respond to the cashier's surly "I'm closed" with a cheery "So is my wallet." Abandon your cart right there (the more items in it, the better) and walk. Why be a victim? There are other supermarkets.

I'VE ALWAYS BELIEVED that unmarked items in supermarkets should be free—or at least subject to negotiation with the cashier. (Marked items that are priced too high may, of course, be placed inside one's coat.) Stores make us suffer enough. Isn't a price break in order?

Don't Blame Me

Dear Mr. Smith:

Every time I bring an unmarked item to the register, the cashier yells "I need a price!" and gives me one of those looks that says "You bad boy, don't you know better than to select something without a sticker?" I always feel like I've done something wrong. (If I know the price and tell her, she doesn't believe me.)

—Innocent of Any Wrongdoing

Dear Innocent:

And the worst part is, you have to wait 10 minutes while some dumbo runs around the store looking for the manager, who also doesn't know the price. No, your time is too valuable. If you have an honest face, tell them you're taking the item with you and here's your phone number—they can call when they know the price and you'll send them a check.

Slow as Molasses

Dear Mr. Smith:

I want to commit murder when I'm on a checkout line and the people ahead of me take too long to pay. Either they wait until the last minute to dig out their wallet, or they fumble around for coupons, or they take another 20 minutes to count out the exact change ("Wait, I've got three cents," they say, and then, on my time, begin to search every crevice but their navel for those stupid pennies). How do I deal with these people?
—*Time Is Money (Mine)*

Dear Time:

Cruelly. If I've had my Recommended Daily Allowance of garlic (7 cloves), I tap them on the shoulder and utter a long-drawn-out "Helloooooooooooooo" when they turn around. This will either a) triple their rate of speed or b) cause them to fall to the floor. A less drastic solution is to be helpful and reach into their wallet or purse, take the money and hand it to the cashier. (Ignore their objections; it's your time they're wasting.)

IN SUPERMARKETS I never speak to strangers—they always want something. Either it's a 4'11" woman asking me to reach that box of prunes on the top shelf and, in the process of stretching, I rip my jacket, or it's someone asking me to save her place in line because she's forgotten pomegranates, or, as the following letter suggests, it's a professional pest. (I will, however, break my vow of silence for a starlet wearing a halter who asks me how to make a rump roast.)

No Good Deed Goes Unpunished

Dear Mr. Smith:

When waiting on a register line, how do I respond when the person behind me asks (and always in such a sweet voice), "I have only these three items, do you mind if I go ahead of you?" I'm also in a hurry, but I'm too timid to say no.

—No More Miss Nice Girl

Dear Reformed:

These people always know who to pick on. There was a time when I'd let them go ahead of me. A man would plead that his car was double-parked; some woman would tell me her water was about to burst. What they didn't tell me was that they had 46 coupons or that they were going to search forever in the bottom of their purse for the exact change. Now, when people tap me on the shoulder and ask to go first, I smile and present them with the following:

MR. SMITH'S FEE SCHEDULE

If You Have:	You May Go Ahead of Me for:
Just one item	75¢
But are going to exchange pleasantries with the cashier	$4.00
2–3 items	$1.25
4–6 items	$2.00
But are going to scrutinize the register tape and ask, "How much did you charge me for the bananas?"	$10.00
7 items or more	$3.50
One of them has to be weighed	$12.00
Something contagious	10¢

"Don't You Have Anything Smaller?"

Dear Mr. Smith:

What do I do about the icy stare I get when I try to pay for an 80¢ purchase with a large bill, as though it's my fault that I didn't first go to the bank and stock up on change?

—Next Time I'll Pay by Check

Dear Next Time:

In the past, when I approached a cashier to pay for a $1.98 item with a $20 bill, I'd get one of those "Don't you have anything smaller?" responses, uttered in a manner suggesting "How dare you not have the exact change?" Then I realized it was not my responsibility to carry a change dispenser on my belt like a Good Humor man. Now, when asked this question, I hold up a quarter and reply, "Is this small enough?"

Carte du Jour

Dear Mr. Smith:

While waiting on line in a supermarket, how do I handle a little old lady who keeps ramming me in the back with her cart? If I say something polite like "Madam, that's the third time you've hit me," she either denies it or tries to look senile. This has occurred more than once.

—Gentle Man

Dear Gentle:

Although they know exactly what they're doing, you must still treat your elders with respect. The next time this happens:

1. Gently (she may be somebody's mother) lift the little old lady.
2. Place her in the shopping cart.
3. Point it toward the frozen foods section.
4. Give the cart a good shove.
5. Pay for your purchases in peace.

Dishonorable (Nasal) Discharge

Dear Mr. Smith:

The other day, this creepy clerk sneezed right in the middle of counting out my change. He didn't say excuse me; he didn't shake out the bills. He just continued to count, ignoring the droplets on George Washington's face. I wanted to ask for different bills, but I hate to make a fuss.

—Getting All Misty

Dear Misty:

And you, of course, catch his cold. This person's a walking epidemic and should be either a) quarantined (place a shopping bag over his head) or b) sterilized (use a boning knife). If this happens again, tell him "Your condition sounds serious" and demand dry money, but, because he's loaded with germs, DON'T LET HIM TOUCH IT! Simply hand him a hankie dipped in chloroform, then, when he drops out of sight, reach into the cash drawer and help yourself.

HEALTH TIP

When taking public transportation, always carry a Pamper to stuff in the mouth of any nearby person who doesn't cover up when he coughs.

Doing Two Things at Once

Dear Mr. Smith:

What do I do when a cashier, while counting out my change, also decides to chat with her co-worker?
—Kept Waiting

Dear Kept:

Isn't it amazing that these people never seem to care that they're inconveniencing you? When this happens to me, I shout as loudly as possible, "MISS, I NEED MY CHANGE BEFORE NOVEMBER!" She instantly comprehends not only that I'm impatient but, even better, that I may be a victim of demonic possession and I get my change instantly—anything to get me off the premises.

ETIQUETTE ADVISORY

When the supermarket cashier is engrossed in reading a magazine and it's your turn to pay,* follow this procedure:

1. Put your groceries on the conveyor belt.
2. If she doesn't acknowledge your presence within 1½ seconds, step behind the register and ring up your purchases. Charge yourself half-price for everything.

* If she's lip-reading, count your change extra carefully.

Check This, Pal

Dear Mr. Smith:

I feel so demeaned when I enter a store and the first words I hear are "Check your bag?" What a way to be greeted. It makes me want to turn around and walk out, especially if it's one of those seamy-looking security guards who looks like he can't wait to fence the contents.
—Above Suspicion

Dear Above:

And then, when you're ready to leave the store, you have to wait while the 14 people in front of you redeem their claim checks. When store security asks, "Check your bag?" I reply, "No thanks, I've already checked it and everything's fine." I then continue on into the store. If they insist, I leave. Why shop where they doubt your honesty?

NOTE: I got back at one particularly insulting establishment (they actually asked me to open my bag on the way out) by checking 10 pounds of warm Stilton and tossing away my claim check.

Pouncers

Dear Mr. Smith:

Is there an effective way to repel assertive sales-people who don't back off when I say "Just looking"? Instead of taking the hint, they hover, breathe down my neck and hit me with "Were you looking for something in particular?" "Yes," I tell them, "a place where I can browse in peace," but they still won't go away.

—Now I Only Window-Shop

Dear Window-Shopper:

Too bad the courts won't issue an order of protection against these people. The moment I enter a store, I ask three questions certain to keep the sales staff away:

1. "Do you have a bathroom?"
2. "Are there any positions available?"
3. "Do you take Mexican money?"

FASHION TIP

At a boutique sale, you may force-fully snatch a garment from the hands of another shopper who's about to try it on if you sincerely believe it will look much better on you.

"DELIVER US FROM EVIL"

▼▼▼

W hy do delivery people refuse to show up when promised? Is it a matter of pride? And why haven't human rights organizations done anything about it? Many correspondents asked how to deal with the homicidal rage that builds up as they watch everyone else on the block get their new couches and washing machines. Call missing persons? Drink? Good choices, but not foolproof. Some alternatives:

Offense

Failure to deliver furniture when promised. You stay home from work, spend the day staring hopefully out the window like a puppy waiting for its mistress, getting excited when you hear a truck, then bursting into tears when it passes your house. You lose one day's pay.

What to Do

Charge the store for your time. If they're unwilling to pay, don't shave or bathe for several weeks, then visit their mattress department. Take lots of naps. (Note: You will not be invited to open a charge account.) If that doesn't work, your only recourse is to enter the store, fall down immediately and sue. (Use my attorney: 1-800-WIPLASH.)

They deliver the wrong item.

Keep it.

Offense	What to Do
They deliver item promised but it was damaged a) in transit or b) while being carelessly squeezed through the door.	Squeeze fat moving man through mail slot—see how he likes it.
Plumber never shows— toilet overflows and causes local flooding.	Leave pail of overflow at plumber's front door.
Bricklayer, carpenter, etc., makes estimate, then leaves, never to be heard from again.	Find out where he lives, show up at dinner time, demand an explanation. (Bring a big friend.)
Doctor doesn't make house calls, you get sicker, then die.	Sue for malpractice.

NOTE: After once spending the month of March at home waiting for a sofa, I visited the offending furniture store, where I asked each customer, "Do you know how many trees they had to cut down to make that coffee table?" I was paid to leave quietly.

Mr. Freddy Is Back

Dear Mr. Smith:

Emergency! This afternoon at the beauty salon, I specifically told my hairdresser "chin length," but either I didn't use the correct word for "chin" (he's Hungarian) or he thought my chin ended at my ear lobes. Now I can't look at myself in the mirror. When I complained, all he had to say was "It'll grow back." I know it will grow back, but not fast enough. I'm going to a party tonight.

—Frantic

Dear Frantic:

Why can't hairdressers apologize when they're wrong, or at least admit human error? (You'd think they worked for the government.) Because a botched hairdo is life-threatening, I suggest you get back at your hairdresser by rendering the ultimate punishment. Take out an ad in the local paper revealing that Luciano's real name is Sydney and that he wears a hairpiece. He'll leave town the same day.

FASHION TIP

Never enter a beauty salon with a sign in the front window announcing "Mr. Giorgio is back" before first finding out where he's been and why he left.

Occupa-
tional
Hazards

▼▼▼

Why do people conspire to make working for a living so much work? Having been fired from 36 jobs, I know what it's like to spend eight hours a day in an office, forced to associate with people unfit, in real life, to call me by my first name: the tyrannical boss who raises his eyebrows when you make a personal call (when his wife calls, act surprised: "Gee, Mrs. ——, I didn't know your husband was married!"), the supervisor who glares at her watch when you go to the bathroom (prove the trip was legitimate: bring back a sample) and co-workers who make your life miserable by a) snapping their gum or b) worse, forcing you to engage in office politics (cure them of these dreadful habits by getting promoted). Alas, I could answer only the worst examples of employee abuse. I do, however, have the following tips for getting even in the workplace. If:

1. *Your boss is a lecher*—Wear something with a revealing neckline. When you catch him staring, file sexual harassment charges.

2. *You're underpaid*—On company time (and expense), either fax several romantic messages to your lonely lover in Singapore or unionize the place.

3. *Your company has mandatory drug testing and you're unable to produce the requisite sample*—Ask the monitor to help. (Careful not to do what one correspondent did in Kalamazoo— he got confused and donated sperm.)

No Rest for the Wary

Dear Mr. Smith:

Help! At the end of the day, just as I'm getting into that "party time" mood, my boss often hands me a pile of work and asks, "Could you possibly get this out tonight?" I can't tell you how many evenings he's ruined.

—Unappreciated Cyndi

Dear Unappreciated:

Besides telling everyone at the company what he earns, there are several ways to rehabilitate a thoughtless boss:

1. If you don't need the job, tell him you're busy and continue your discussion on the phone about where to meet your friend for happy hour. (Also hand him a mirror and tell him to hold it steady while you apply your lipstick.)

2. If you need the job, make his life miserable:

▲ Put through all calls, especially those that are a) from his ex-wife and b) alimony-related; or

▲ Leave his tuna salad sandwich out in the sun (for best results, make sure it's green); or

▲ Take maternity leave.*

---

* You need not be pregnant. Enlightened corporations grant six weeks' maternity leave to any woman who promises to use the time productively—to find a husband.

Slave Trade

Dear Mr. Smith:

As an executive assistant, I feel it diminishes me when my boss sends me on her personal errands. Last week I had to pick up a dress she'd had altered, yesterday I was sent to buy a gift for her husband and just now I found a note on my desk asking me to be her rep at a funeral. I wasn't hired to be a domestic.

—Mike

Dear Mike:

Just hope she doesn't ask you to sleep with her husband, too. The following flow chart may be helpful.

To Cure a Boss of:	*Course of Action*
Sending you on personal errands—food shopping, getting her car serviced, retrieving her cat from the vet, renting an adult movie for the weekend, etc.	Take as long as possible, like the entire day. This lets you catch up on your personal life—see a movie, pick up your laundry, go on a job interview, visit friends, etc. (When you finally return, tell her the traffic was brutal.)

To Cure a Boss of:	*Course of Action*
Asking you to buy gifts for her mother, children, business associates, maid or husband	Use your own (warped) judgment. A little something for her mom? Purchase a gift certificate to a drug rehabilitation center. Some token of appreciation for an important business client? Buy a puppy. Something fashionable for her husband to wear? Culottes.*
Timing you when you use the bathroom	Keep a bedpan by your desk.
Making you get coffee	Never get it right. She takes it black? Stuff it with cream. Unsweetened? Dump in 30 sugars.
Making an inappropriate sexual advance (not technically an "errand" but relevant)	Respond.

* Or a "Will work for beer" T-shirt.

ETIQUETTE ADVISORY

When your boss gives you money for your purchases, it is proper to keep the change.

"Here's Looking at You"

Dear Mr. Smith:

How do I handle a co-worker who barges into my office to show me photos of her daughter's new baby? I couldn't care less, but I don't want to offend her so I "ooh" and "ah" over 37 pictures that are a) blurry and b) all the same, a feat of diplomacy that sorely taxes my social skills. Any guidelines?

—Captive Audience of One

Dear Captive:

These are the same people who make you sit through hours of wedding and vacation pictures, none of which, to relieve the boredom, contain frontal nudity. Make the situation tolerable either by:

1. Removing your reading glasses. This saves not only your eyesight, but also your sanity; or

2. Getting your fingerprints all over the photos. You'll not be bothered again.

PHOTO FINISH

I myself am unable to put on a happy face when forced to admire several photos of an infant that looks more like a diapered Gouda. I repay my tormentor by showing (very slowly) all 15 pictures I carry of Billy, my parakeet, taking a nap.

A Waist Is a Terrible Thing to Mind

Dear Mr. Smith:

My wife, the senior vice president of a huge conglomerate, is up for a terrific promotion and wants to invite her boss over for dinner. He is, unfortunately, a man of size (5'7", 273 pounds), and most of our furniture consists of rather fragile period antiques. I'm sure he'll expect to dine sitting up—any ideas?
—Nervous About Our Windsor Chairs

Dear Nervous:

I understand—our neighbor just broke our porch swing. Either:

1. Do a picnic and dine alfresco (he can't possibly break your lawn); or

2. Hide your Duncan Phyfes and be diplomatic: engrave B.Y.O.C. (Bring Your Own Chair) on the dinner invitation.

I Give (and Give) at the Office

Dear Mr. Smith:

Lately it seems that after deductions for taxes, FICA and office collections, I have little left over to feed my children. Whenever I look up from my desk, there's a co-worker with her hand out. Last month there were solicitations for:

▲ *Clyde's retirement*

▲ *Andrea's farewell party*

▲ *Lola's baby shower*

▲ *The football pool*

▲ *A gift for Harriet's birthday*

▲ *The engagement of someone I'm positive doesn't even work here*

Half these people I hardly know. The other half I don't like that much. I'm going broke.

Bankrupt

Dear Bankrupt:

And it's always that same perky do-gooder who does the collecting. (Are these people ever audited?) When they come around, I tell them either:

1. "See me tomorrow" (particularly effective if it's Friday afternoon); or

2. "You contribute for me—I'll pay you back later" (certain to make them turn ashen and flee).

Don't Tread on Me

▼▼▼

I'm puzzled by the idea of social responsibility. To whom should we be responsible? Have things gone too far? Must we, as we hand over our wallet to a mugger, inquire about his troubled childhood? (Only if he's still wearing short pants.) "I should know better than to ask for justice," began one letter written by a little old lady, currently under indictment for attempting to rehabilitate a mugger with a skillet. (Her assailant is being "counseled.") No wonder most of us walk around hiding behind earphones and sunglasses.

This section is for the truly disadvantaged members of society, ordinary citizens whose right to peace is continually challenged by rag-wielding windshield washers (I've no problem allowing someone to wash my windshield, so long as he does it while the car's in motion); cyclists who ride their bike on the sidewalk (and into my shins—inserting a stick between their wheel spokes is adequate retribution); and obsessed activists who block your path to promote their cause. Why aren't these people at work? (Frontier justice tip: Instantly stop the most rabid zealot by pressing an orbital sander to his nose.)

For the woman "Without a Song" in Providence, Rhode Island, I have this advice: replace that wimpy "Sorry No Radio" sign in the window of your BMW (in thieves this merely arouses contempt) with something more inspirational like "Nothing in this car is worth losing your life over." On the seat place a wild-eyed pit bull who's already gnawed through half your steering wheel.

ARE YOU YOUR BROTHER'S KEEPER?

▼▼▼

How to cope with annoying panhandlers? There were hundreds of letters asking how much to give and when to give. I can't offer monetary advice—the cost of living varies so throughout the United States. Fifty cents might be generous in Tupelo, Mississippi, but on the streets of Manhattan anything less than your paycheck (endorsed) will get you cursed or chased. Some rules:

1. Never give money to anyone who a) dresses better, b) looks healthier or c) has more hair than you do.

2. Never give money to anyone who looks able-bodied (i.e., is capable of doing a day's work or at least studying the want ads). Exception: talented street musicians.

3. Never give money to people who call themselves "disenfranchised." It means they have a social worker.

4. If you feel extra-charitable, give your money with no strings attached. Certainly it would be nice to see your hard-earned cash spent on healthy items like pea soup and galoshes, but some people think of cigarettes and wine as comfort food—it's not fair to disillusion them.

5. Don't be too quick to drop loose change into just any jiggling cup . . . it might be someone's coffee.

Identity Crisis

Dear Mr. Smith

I'm an Afro-American who recently emigrated from Chicago to Africa. Here in Kenya, when people ask, I never know what to call myself. I've tried "Americo-African" but get curious stares. Any suggestions?

—Confused

Dear Confused:

What happened to patriotism? Why can't Americans refer to themselves as "American" instead of using hyphens? It's un-American and schizophrenic. A friend who's half Filipino and half Chinese calls herself Fil-Chi-American; her boyfriend, who's half British and half Assyrian, describes himself as Brit-Ass-American; and a neighborhood activist, part Mongolian and part Hong Kongese, insists on being called Mong-Kong-American. I realize we're all proud of our heritage, but wouldn't it be more fun to make people guess our ethnic origins— possibly by nose size, or (more scientifically) how spicy we take our food? For those with an identity crisis and reluctant to call themselves merely "American," I offer the following guide to correct ethnic terminology.

If You Are a Mixture of:	*Refer to Yourself as:*
Latvian and Lithuanian	Latlith
Finnish and Chinese	Finchin
Spanish and German	Spangerm
Hungarian and Polish	Hungpole
English and Scotch	Englotch
Native American (Navaho) and Maltese	Navamalt
French and Greek	Freek
Samoan and Panamanian	Sampan
Black and Jewish	Bluish
Norwegian and Pakistani	Norpak
Persian and Turkish	Perkish
Japanese and Laplander	Japlap
Italian and Icelandic	Italic

"Hold It!"

Dear Mr. Smith:

So often when I'm on an elevator and it's about to leave, someone rushes up and tries to insert his hand between the closing doors. If I'm pressed for time, is it okay to whack his fingers with my umbrella?

—Tim Waits for No Man

Dear Tim:

First ask, "What's the password?" If he doesn't know it, you may then whack his fingers.

CONFIDENTIAL TO "HATES DO-GOODERS" IN HOLLYWOOD: The Good Samaritan who is already on your elevator and holding the door for stragglers is being a nice guy on your valuable time. Shove him out of the car and immediately press the "Close" button. There's nothing like that warm-all-over feeling of satisfaction when you hear him pounding in rage on the closed doors.

ELEVATOR SELF-DEFENSE

▼▼▼

Many people have asked what to do when other passengers on their elevator want to "communicate." You prefer to be alone with your thoughts or enjoy your grouchy mood, but they want to talk about the weather or comment on the book you've carefully buried your nose in. Such pests can be instantly discouraged by doing one, or all, of the following:

1. Stare hard at your shoes.

2. Lip-read the elevator inspection certificate.

3. Face the rear.

4. Curl up in a corner and take a short nap (Best Bet).

5. Wear a ski mask.

6. Smile and ask, "Have you been saved?"

Criminal Loitering

Dear Mr. Smith:

What do I do if I'm waiting to use the cash machine and the people in front of me are taking too long to finish?

—I Rate

Dear I Rate:

If you find them attractive, make the time pass pleasantly by massaging their necks. If not, penalize them by either running off with their packages or doing something creepy . . . like blowing in their ear. If, of course, you have theater tickets and are worried about arriving late, simply explain that it's an emergency, pick them up and move them aside.* If they're slow-witted, they won't even notice.

---

* Courtesy tip: Put them back in front of the machine when you're done.

Dodge City

Dear Mr. Smith:

Why do pedestrians think they own the crosswalk, particularly when I'm in a rush to deliver a pizza? There's always that one thoughtless person who tries to scamper across at the last minute, just as my light's turning green. Do I really have to wait until he's clear of my vehicle?

—Love Those Jackrabbit Starts

Dear Jack:

Not if a) you're in a hurry and b) you need a new hood ornament. The rule is simple:

1. If the offender makes a sincere effort to quickly step out of your way, be merciful and wait.

2. If he's intentionally dawdling, teach him a lesson: floor it and watch him scramble. (You are under no obligation to stop your vehicle and help a pedestrian pick up his parcels.)

POINT OF MOTORIST ETIQUETTE

When the light changes to green, even if it will slow you down, try to go around any pedestrian who is caught in the crosswalk—especially if he falls to his knees and pleads for his life.

Beep? Bop.

Dear Mr. Smith:

What do I do when I'm stopped at a light and the instant it changes to green, the person behind me blows his horn? It's maddening.

—Silence Is Golden

Dear Silence:

I am, of course, against violence, but these are the very drivers who deserve to be pulled from their car and pummeled. They lower the quality of our lives and have to be reeducated. Before I discovered it was unlawful, I'd put my car in reverse and floor it, a procedure that instantly let the hornblower know I was annoyed. (Auto insurance paid for my trunk.) Now I simply exit my vehicle, grasp the hornblower's ear, lift the hood of his car, tape his ear to the horn, then blow it according to the following guidelines:

If Offender Sounded Horn Because:	*I Blow Horn for:*
I didn't accelerate the instant the light turned green.	1 minute
My engine momentarily stalled.	20 minutes

I dared allow an ailing senior citizen, caught in the crosswalk when the light changed, to hobble back to safety on the sidewalk.

8 minutes (9 minutes if the senior is using an aluminum walker)

I was daydreaming.

11 minutes

He was speeding on coffee.

25 minutes

He knows me.

5 minutes

THE PROPER THING

It is proper to sound one's horn under extraordinary circumstances:

1. When a cute guy goes by.

2. To let your date know you've arrived to pick her up, it's raining, and you don't feel like getting out of the car.

3. When passing a hospital zone . . . those patients sleep too much.

4. If you're a Type A personality and the motorist in front of you is:

a) Taking too long to pay the toll.

b) Asking the toll-taker for directions.

5. When you want to test the reflexes of the service station attendant who's checking your oil.

Engine Block

Dear Mr. Smith:

Recently, when I parked my car on the street, I returned to find it blocked in by a double-parked vehicle. I would have blown my horn, but I'm too considerate. After an hour, the owner finally showed up and completely ignored me—just got into his car and drove off without an apology. I was furious. Next time I'll get even, but how?

—Steaming

Dear Steaming:

I know that feeling—you want to smash his window, release the brake and roll the car down the street. In some of the more medieval parts of the United States, however, this is still unlawful. Instead:

1. Wait for the owner—on the roof of his car. If you carry chalk, pass the time productively by practicing your hopscotch technique.

2. Call a garage, explain that you locked yourself out of "your" car and have it towed, far away.

3. a) Lift the hood of the offending vehicle.
   b) Sell the contents to passing motorists.

Aching Feet

Dear Mr. Smith:

Why are all the best parking spaces reserved for the handicapped? Most of the time they're empty, anyway— is our nation getting healthier? I've wasted hours driving around our mall, determined to park in at least the same zip code as the Wal-Mart's. What would entitle me to a "Handicapped Only" space?

—Stalled at the Mall

Dear Stalled:

If you're hesitant about using a Handicapped Only space, take your pulse . . . if it's erratic, pull in. Otherwise, use one of these justifications:

▲ Wearing stiletto heels—unable to walk more than 100 feet without wobbling.

▲ Just returning a refrigerator— won't be but a minute or two.

▲ Spring fever.

▲ Feminine itching.

CONFIDENTIAL TO "SPECIAL EXCEPTION" IN PALO ALTO:
"Handicapped" refers to people, not vehicles. Driving a jalopy with bad rust spots and leaking oil does not entitle you to a handicapped space.

Coddle Eggs, Not Criminals

Dear Mr. Smith:

Although they caught the person who mugged me, he got only two years. This means that with time off for a) time already served and b) good behavior, he'll be on the street by, let's see . . . 6 P.M. I'm told that short sentences are the rule because of prison "overcrowding." Instead of wasting our tax dollars on more prisons, how about incarcerating thinner convicts?

—Ex-Liberal

Dear Ex:

Don't feel bad. Because my mugger wore a suit, they called it a white-collar crime and fined him $50, for which his friends held a fund raiser—they mugged a little old lady. Instead of jail, which turns ho-hum thieves into super criminals, there are other, more enlightened punishments:

1. For first offenders:

Choice A (Manhattan only)—Cleaning the subways. (Discipline problems would be given the privilege of mopping the third rail.)

Choice B—Community service (stringing Christmas lights—while wearing wet boots).

2. For second-, third- and fourth-time male offenders: a sex-change operation. (Women are easier to rehabilite.)

THE MACE STATUTES

▼▼▼

"**W**hen stopped at a red light, may I use Mace to repel someone who's wiping the window of my Lexus with a filthy squeegee?" writes a lady from Manhattan. Mace? What is the world coming to? As a nonviolent person, I've always believed in reasoning with pests (exception: vacuum cleaner salesmen). Yet many of you, tired of feeling defenseless, asked about the propriety of using Mace or a similar substance such as pepper spray or Cool Whip. The rule is simple. Use a spray device:

1. To quickly get rid of:
▲ Muggers
▲ Any waiter or waitress who tries to remove your plate before you've finished eating
▲ Mr. Wrong
▲ Aggressive panhandlers
▲ Sniffing dogs
▲ Anyone who approaches you at an airport who is wearing a long orange robe and is not a long-lost relative
▲ Paparazzi
▲ Co-workers with poor personal hygiene
2. To express displeasure toward surly civil servants (You are, after all, paying their salary.)
3. Any shopper in the "50% Off" section of a boutique who is reaching for the same garment as you.

Bull's-Eye

Dear Mr. Smith:

Is shooting a fleeing burglar ever justified? The other day, after hearing a strange noise, I ran to my living room just in time to see a man racing from the house with my new 27-inch Sony. I wanted to get my rifle, but my wife said I'd be violating his constitutional rights. Instead, she said, I should chase him. Well, sir, I'm too fat to chase anyone. All I know is, my television set is gone and I have to spend my evenings making conversation.

—No More (sob) MTV

Dear Deprived:

Before taking the law into your own hands, you must first, as he's running away, offer to buy back the TV. If he ignores you:

1. Make an effort: at least *try* to chase him while shouting, "Stop, thief."
2. If you're really out of shape, yell, "Slow down, thief."
3. If this doesn't work, fire a warning shot above his head.
4. If he continues to run, fire another warning shot, this time below his head.*

---

* Among criminologists, this is known as "Instant Rehabilitation."

Fed Up

▼▼▼

Eaters beware: once you leave home and the security of your stove and refrigerator, you put your appetite in the hands of others, like the host who first seats you next to a bore, then serves a squab the size of a wren, causing you, for the first time in your life, to face starvation. In a restaurant, of course, you must depend on the kindness of strangers, like the maître d' who, if you're not a rock star, puts you at a table only slightly larger than a coaster and the waiter who speed-talks as he recites the specials of the day, then gets testy when you ask him to repeat them.

Is there any way to protect yourself? Well . . . yes. If you're going to a restaurant, bring a change of clothing in case they have a dress code. If you're going to a dinner party, a) bring a cellular phone in case the other guests aren't as amusing as yourself, and b) if it's refrigerated, your glove compartment is the perfect place to store a midnight snack should the host not furnish doggie bags.

Although many of you asked for help, I felt,

because this is a family etiquette manual, it would
be tasteless to reproduce the more extreme
letters. I therefore omitted correspondence from
"Impatient in Burbank" asking whether, if the
waiter doesn't bring the check fast enough, it's
okay to get up and leave without paying (yes) and
"Breathless in Boise," who wanted to know about
the propriety of discouraging a smoker from lighting an after-dinner cigar by pouring soup over it.
(I recommend minestrone.)

"**I**S IT PROPER to repel at knife point an overzealous waiter who tries to remove my plate before I'm finished eating?" . . . "What are we in for, Mr. Smith, when our waiter introduces himself by name?" This was the general tone of the letters from leery restaurant patrons who, instead of enjoying a pleasant dining experience, often found themselves victimized by the very person sworn to serve them.

Parlez-Vous Français?

Dear Mr. Smith:

Being neither multicultural nor multilingual, I always feel intimidated in French restaurants— particularly when the menu is 80% French, the waiter is 90% condescending and the patrons are thin. Should I just throw myself on the waiter's mercy?

—Tongue-Tied

Dear Tongue-Tied:

Being mean is inexcusable. I always put French waiters in their place by demanding their green card and more bread while I'm being led to my table. If the waiter is patronizing because a) you keep asking for menu translations or b) you can't say "ratatouille provençal" without losing your dentures, exercise your rights. When he asks if everything's all right, smile, then knock him senseless with your lamb chop and, when the check arrives, take out your calculator and ask, "Oh, garçon, is there a French word for 'Une teensy tip'?"

RESTAURANT TIPPING

▼▼▼

Tipping can express displeasure as well as pleasure. A dawdling waiter, for instance, who doesn't bring drinks quickly enough, gets only 8% of the check (5¼% if I'm really thirsty). A waitress who leaves in the middle of my meal because she has an audition gets 6%. Below are some additional guidelines.

If:	Of the Check, Tip Only:
▲ To obtain the waiter's attention I have to clink my knife against my glass or my companion's forehead	11%
▲ The waiter gives me a surly look when I don't order a drink	13%
▲ The waiter tells me his name	7%
Without my asking him	3%
▲ The waiter rolls his eyes when I ask, "Is the flounder fresh?"	12%
▲ The waiter keeps asking:	
"Is everything okay?"	14%
"Is anything okay?"	2%
▲ Though the restaurant's nearly empty, my girlfriend and I are denied a roomy table ("Sorry, it's reserved for a party of four") and made to dine in torture on a surface only slightly larger than a coin	7%

▲ I was brought an absurdly small
portion and the waiter failed to
apologize 10%

▲ I have evidence that, in the kitchen,
the waiter dropped my chicken Kiev
on the floor and, instead of getting
another one, cleaned it with Lestoil 5%

▲ I had to prevent a compulsive waiter
from making off with a bottle
containing one last precious swig
of Heineken by rapping his knuckles
with the sugar bowl 13%

▲ The waiter takes forever to bring
the check and I'm desperate to
just go home and go to sleep................................10%

▲ The waiter asks if he can use my
Visa card...1%

THE PROPER THING

Secretaries' luncheon only: If waiter is very handsome and flirts, increase his tip by 5% . . . or 8%
if he has rich black hair and an Italian accent.

Free Spirits

Dear Mr. Smith:

I think the prices restaurants charge for drinks are outrageous. They're entitled to a profit, but $6 for a martini? $4 for a 70¢ bottle of beer? $20 for a $5 bottle of wine? Have these people no shame?

—Insolvent

Dear Insolvent:

You forgot the $3 for that absurd little bottle of mineral water. I used to enter these places with my hands in the air—resigned to being robbed. Now I observe these three rules:

1. Bring a flask of your favorite spirits, order one drink and add to it discreetly—your waiter will never guess why it takes you two hours to finish a martini.

2. Never order wine unless:
   a) You're on an expense account; or
   b) You have a sworn statement that your companion is picking up the check.

3. Always order tap water. Mineral water causes gallstones.

NOTE: I once thought "House Wine" meant wine you brought from your house. Sommeliers were never amused, however, when I withdrew a $3 bottle of Bulgarian chablis from under my coat.

ALL-YOU-CAN-EAT BUFFETS AND SALAD BARS

▼▼▼

"C an I really eat all I want?" asked one correspondent, who said she felt intimidated by the stares of other diners (and the owner) when she went back for her seventh helping of breaded shrimp. The following guidelines will help.

1. Never feel guilty about going back for more. (When questioned, explain that you have multiple personalities and must feed them all.)

2. Wear loose clothing; it'll make it easier to reach under the sneeze guard. I recommend a shower curtain.

3. Make every trip count. To get more food on your plate, tamp the potatoes down with the heel of your shoe.

4. Be sure you get your money's worth. In dim lighting, it's easy to overlook the beets.

5. Many restaurants offer an overwhelming choice of salad dressings. If you're uncertain, dip your fingertip in each one to help you decide.

6. Survival tip for the weary: pull your chair over and eat directly from the buffet table. This saves trips.

7. Don't forget a midnight snack. On your last trip to the buffet table, stuff a few sausages into your pocket.

Tie-Land?

Dear Mr. Smith:

When entering a restaurant, I sometimes see a sign that says "Proper Attire Required." What does "proper attire" mean?

—Slave of Fashion

Dear Slave:

That you're going to pay $25 for a $5 piece of fish* and, if you're not wearing a jacket, the restaurant will supply you with a one-size-fits-all coat that's been previously worn by who-knows-how-many bacteria-laden patrons. (If it fits, and you like the cut, take it home. I myself possess an enviable collection of Nehru jackets.) It's bad enough having dress codes at work—why must we be plagued when we relax? For those daunted by dress restrictions, my personal guidelines combine eating in comfort with looking presentable:

If It's:	*"Proper Attire" Means:*
A health-food restaurant	Bicycle pants
A rib place	Overalls and mittens
Gourmet seafood	Waders and a lobster bib

* And that their kitchen plays host to a better class of mice.

If It's:	*"Proper Attire" Means:*
A chic bistro (no shorts allowed)	Take them off
Chinese	Something low-cut to catch the rice that falls off your chopsticks
French	A credit card
Hungarian	Pajamas and house slippers (goulash makes me sleepy)
Italian	
Northern	Casual slacks
Southern	Elastic-waist pants (the portions are larger)
Spanish	Sweat pants (to better contain escaping gas)
All-you-can-eat buffet	A wet suit

Rain Check

Dear Mr. Smith:

Does "Restrooms for patrons only" apply to me? These signs appear at the least opportune moments, like when I'm passing a restaurant and suddenly have to go. Are they worried I'll wear out their precious porcelain? What if I promise only to wash my hands?

—Indignant

Dear Indignant:

Why don't Human Rights activists protest this kind of torture? I never hesitate to enter a restaurant and use the facilities. If they object, I mention that when I last ate there I didn't use their bathroom, so they owe me a visit. (I could also say that I'm meeting a friend for lunch and could I use the restroom while I'm waiting? I cannot, however, tell a lie.)

THE PROPER THING

In America, only the words "Men" and "Women" should be used on a restaurant's bathroom door. Why should we have to stand before a door labeled HOMMES or FRAUEN and anxiously wonder whether we're about to enter a men's room, a ladies' room or a utility closet?

They Also Wait Who Only Stand and Serve

Dear Mr. Smith:

Have you ever been with a dinner companion who can't decide what to order? I sit there starving, frantically stuffing my face with bread sticks, while she leisurely studies the menu and interrogates the waiter: "Is there a lot of pepper on the steak au poivre? How do you prepare the grilled red snapper? From what country are your country-style ribs?" Then she'll announce, "I need more time," as the waiter lowers his pencil, rolls his eyes and walks away. I always know instantly what I want. Why doesn't she?

—Decisive

Dear Decisive:

Are you sure you're not dining with a bureaucrat? In a restaurant, if my companion takes more than a minute to make up her mind, I assume she needs a therapist, not a waiter, and order for myself. What if the kitchen runs out of food? Just because two people enter a restaurant together doesn't mean they have to eat together.*

---

* A whispered "Last one to finish pays the check" will encourage your companion to order more quickly.

On-Time Departures

Dear Mr. Smith:

The other night at a popular restaurant, the hostess promised my wife and me a really nice table "just as soon as the people sitting there pay their check and leave, which should be shortly." Even though the people saw we were waiting, they lingered at the table, taking mini-sips of their espresso, laughing and enjoying themselves—while we starved! Worse, when they finally paid their check, instead of getting up instantly, they continued to talk. How might we have hastened their departure?

—Next Time Taco Bell

Dear Taco:

That white heat in the pit of your stomach is what I call fury at having to a) wait while these people nonchalantly linger over coffee at your personal table and b) watch waiters rush by carrying plates of food destined for everyone but you. You have three choices:

▲ *Polite*—Walk up to the table, tell the people sitting there you're hungry and ask them to leave.

▲ *More polite*—Introduce yourselves, then sit down and join their conversation.

▲ *Very polite*—Walk up to the table and stand there looking wretched and hungry. Emphasize your misery by lowering your tongue until the tip makes contact with their cheesecake.

——

CONFIDENTIAL TO "FEEL VIOLATED" IN OAKLAND: When dining out, you should feel irritated when people at the next table stare at your food. Next they'll be asking for a taste!* I used to solve this problem diplomatically, either by covering my Lamb Osso Buco with a tea cozy or keeping my plate where they couldn't see it—on my lap. Now I simply write "Order some of these, they're great" on a French fry and flip it at the starers. I give myself extra points if it lands in a wine glass.**

✱ If you do allow a taste, decide on portion size and be sure to dole it out yourself.
✱✱ Alternate solution: summon the waiter and send yourself a bottle of champagne—compliments of the starers.

H AVING RECENTLY spent an evening in a restaurant doing two things at once (eating a bowl of fettuccine Alfredo while listening to a crying child at the next table), I feel restaurants should be more discriminating about who they allow in. If your meal is being ruined by a squalling toddler, demand a rebate and a drink. Dress codes aren't enough. Perhaps we need a child code.

Unwelcome Intrusion

Dear Mr. Smith:

Have restaurants become day-care centers? While trying to enjoy a quiet dinner, my husband and I had to endure an infant at the next table. Not only was he throwing a tantrum, but the parents were doing nothing to shut him up. Pelting the kid with pats of butter only made him scream louder.

—Childless and Thrilled

Dear Fortunates:

When I become the dictator, children under 10 will not be permitted in restaurants—you never know when they're going to go off. If the parents don't have the consideration to give the kid a bottle and check him with their coats, or send him to other tables to forage for food, you should be compensated for your misery. Dinner's on Baby—as you're leaving, tuck the check into his diaper.*

✱ Less subtle but more effective:
1. *Vulgar*—Light up a Dunhill and blow cigar smoke at the table.
2. *Wonderfully vulgar*—Compromise. If they'll lower Baby's volume, you'll stop flossing while they try to enjoy their shrimp in lobster sauce.

Surprise!

Dear Mr. Smith:

Last week, as my wife and I were enjoying a quiet meal in our favorite restaurant, a waiter suddenly emerged from the kitchen with a cake and pandemonium broke loose—10 people at the next table began to sing "Happy Birthday" with a vigor that collapsed my chocolate soufflé. It ruined our meal.

—Ears Still Ringing

Dear Victim of a Choral Society:

You should know better than to patronize a restaurant that doesn't provide a "No Singing" section. The first four letters of restaurant spell "rest." The only loud noise you should tolerate is that of a champagne cork popping or someone saying, "Drinks are on the house." If you make this mistake again, know that you have certain rights:

1. You do not have to sing along.

2. You are entitled, after the candles are blown out, to reach over and help yourself to a fistful of cake.*

---

* And might I suggest a class-action suit by you and the other angry patrons.

Check Mate?

Dear Mr. Smith:

Whenever we eat out with a certain couple, they're always "distracted" when the bill arrives. Either he runs to the bathroom or she's at the dessert cart taking Polaroids for her scrapbook. Last night I paid again. (As we were leaving the restaurant, emboldened by wine and my daughter's tuition bill, I said, "Your share comes to $74.25." "That sounds right," he replied, then bade us good night.) My fiancée says that when the check arrives I, too, should go to the bathroom, but that's cowardly and unsanitary. Any suggestions?

—No Re-Treat

Dear No Re-Treat:

Only amateurs make the mistake of acknowledging a dinner check when it arrives. My policy is to a) never make eye contact with the check and b) be patient—cheap dinner companions must be outwaited. When the bill arrives, I open my copy of *The Wall Street Journal* and study stock listings until, from across the table, I hear a credit card sliding out of a wallet. If this doesn't work, I tear the check in two, hand over the bottom half and say, "Let's split it."*

---

* Murmuring "I'll get our coats" and bolting for the checkroom the moment the bill arrives has been known to work.

CONFIDENTIAL TO "NEVER AGAIN" IN ROANOKE: Hint that it's your friend's turn to pay by gently leaning over and blowing the check toward his plate.

WHO PAYS FOR DRINKS?

▼▼▼

Y ou have 8 P.M. reservations at your favorite restaurant, but when you get there the maître d' announces there'll be a short wait for your table (translation: 25 minutes) and graciously "invites" you to have a drink at the bar. Who pays for this drink? Silly me. I once thought that because the maître d' asked so nicely, it was his treat. I learned differently, however, when, after handing him our bar check, he took a swing at me.

My new policy: If the delay is our fault (we arrive a half-hour late), I pay. If it's their fault (the maître d' is too fainthearted to walk over to our still-occupied table and turn their chairs upside down), the restaurant pays.

Bottle Fatigue

Dear Mr. Smith:

What do I do at a wine tasting when I'm with my so-called "connoisseur" friends? They'll take a sip, tilt their heads back and emit wine-friendly sounds like "What body" . . . "Perfect balance" . . . "Elegantly firm" . . . "An admirable counterpoint to the soft-shelled crabs." When I take a sip, tilt my head back and exclaim, "Yummy, gimme some more," they put me down for acting like a peasant—even if I cover my mouth when I burp.

—Sluggo

Dear Sluggo:

Don't be intimidated by the so-called experts. They just feel guilty about getting drunk. When tasting wine, first let a little run down the side of your mouth just to show you're not a snob, dab your chin with your tie, lick the cork, then utter one of the following phrases for:

▲ *Any red*—"Noble, with just the hint of oak."

▲ *Any white*—"Soft and flinty, delightfully approachable. Where are my Tums?"

▲ *A blush or rosé*—"Perfect for my next pool party."

▲ *Any restaurant house wine*—"Well-crafted, and you needn't make a face when swallowing."

▲ *Any wine you're not sure of*—"It matches my shirt."

P ROFESSIONAL GUESTS know there are only five reasons to attend a
dinner party: 1) to eat; 2) to drink; 3) to be merry; 4) to gossip; 5) to
leave with a better umbrella. An exhausting regimen indeed. Yet there
are hosts who demand more, making even the most generous guest want
to bite the hand that feeds him.

Open Sesame?

Dear Mr. Smith:

*Being a klutz, I was concerned when, at a formal
dinner, the host asked me to open a bottle of frighten-
ingly expensive burgundy (Romanée-Conti '66). I tried
to beg off,* but he was adamant. (Why do people insist
that you do their job?) Naturally, the cork broke off in
the bottle, and I had to use a screwdriver to pry the rest
of it out. When I then pursed my lips and sipped directly
from the bottle to eliminate the cork crumbs, two women
fainted and the host began to hyperventilate. Next time,
how do I graciously decline?*

—Resourceful

Dear Resourceful:

By asking, as you begin to insert the corkscrew, the
question that will make the host snatch the bottle from
your hands:
"How hard must I shake it?"

---

* "Twisting a corkscrew throws out my back" is an acceptable excuse.

Night-Care Center

Dear Mr. Smith:

How do you handle dinner guests who can't get a baby-sitter (or so they say) and show up with a super-manic five-year-old totally wired on Pepsi and chocolate? He nearly destroyed the evening.

—Still Stewing

Dear Still:

When this happens, simply explain there's no extra food, give the kid some Legos and let him play in the garage. If you feel this is ungenerous, offer a Shirley Temple made with two parts orange juice and 10 parts Nyquil; encourage tyke to sip slowly. He'll sleep soundly under the piano bench for the entire evening.

THE PROPER THING

Guests have also been known to show up with their dog, usually one that is perilously incontinent. Should this happen, it's permissible to place Fido in a garment bag until they leave.

The Lonely Eater

Dear Mr. Smith:

What can I do at a dinner party when the people on either side of me turn away and become absorbed in conversation with their neighbors? It makes me a) feel left out and b) wonder about my breath.

—Ostracized

Dear Ostracized:

Regain their attention by asking them to cut your meat. If this doesn't work, take the opportunity, while they're ignoring you, to:

1. Eat their food and drink their wine; or
2. Make bread pellets and flip them at your host; or
3. Thumb through your Filofax; or
4. Toss scraps to the family dog; or
5. Ask that a phone be brought to your table; or
6. Stand up, clink your knife against your glass and auction off your spouse.

THE PROPER THING

If it's been a long day, this is your chance to prepare for dessert by lowering your head onto your plate and taking a nap.

One for the Road

Dear Mr. Smith:

After a dinner party, if I've brought the host an expensive gift but don't feel I've gotten my money's worth, is it proper to ask for a doggie bag?

—Bashful

Dear Bashful:

Yes, and who cares that she was hoarding the extra food for her kids' lunches? So often, because I was too proud to ask, I've left dinner parties still starving, wishing I'd had the courage to ask for the remaining lasagna, some garlic bread and a slice of that apple pie the hostess had already put away (and much too soon, if you ask me). Now what I do is volunteer to clear the table and, when no one's looking, quickly stuff my face with leftovers. (I have the God-given ability to swallow a chicken pot pie whole, without choking.)

COCKTAIL PARTY SURVIVAL

▼▼▼

Because my sanity is more important than being "polite," the term "party hopping" has always meant jumping up and down on the feet of anyone who corners me and sprays bits of olive loaf on my lapels as he asks me what I do. Below are some party survival strategies should you find yourself trapped by a bore.

Do Not:

Smile and nod pleasantly as he discusses his Inner Child—you'll be well into your golden years before he shuts up.

Hesitate, if you're desperate, to silence him by wiping a tuna purée hors d'oeuvre across his forehead.

Try to escape by asking him to get you a drink. He'll hunt you down no matter where you are (even in the bathroom).

Give him your phone number.

Do:

Prepare to get rid of him by waving occasionally to a potted plant across the room and mouthing "See you in a minute."

If you can afford it, hire a nurse to hover nearby and murmur warnings that you're overdoing it.

Seek relief by dropping to your hands and knees and crawling through the legs of other guests until you reach safety.

Give him your zip code.

Not Even a Doggie Bag?

Dear Mr. Smith:

I always hear about convicted criminals expressing "remorse" for some horrible crime they've committed. The nearer their execution date, the more remorse they express, along with how they've changed and how it's wrong for the state to take a life (theirs, in particular). I, however, believe in capital punishment. Not only does it ease the emotional pain of the victim's relatives and express society's outrage, but it also relieves prison overcrowding. Recently, when I expressed this view at a dinner party, the host (a liberal, I guess) got extremely upset and asked me to leave, right in the middle of my roast beef. Do you think he acted properly?

—Starving

Dear Starving:

Your host overreacted (probably has a relative sitting on death row). You have a right to go back and demand a) the rest of your roast beef, b) dessert and c) an apology.

They Lied

Dear Mr. Smith:

When invited to a friend's house for dinner, I showed my appreciation by bringing a very expensive bottle of wine. She said, "You shouldn't have," so I didn't—I took the wine with me when I left. I haven't heard from her in three years. What happened?

—Stumped

Dear Stumped:

You took her too literally. When a guest arrives at my dinner party clutching a bottle of wine, I grab it, immediately inspect the label and, if it's too good to share, put the wine aside to savor after everyone's gone. (Or, if I can't wait, I take it into the bathroom and sneak sips while everyone's on their main course.)

POINT OF ETIQUETTE

When asked to dinner, play it safe: don't bring the host anything. Afterwards, if the food was good, show your appreciation by sending flowers ($15). If the food was bad, just send a thank-you note (29¢).

Bring 'Em Back Alive

Dear Mr. Smith:

I'm so upset. Last week, after I spent two intense days preparing an elaborate dinner party (chopping mint leaves for the Mediterranean lamb stew was exhausting), our guests called at the last minute and canceled. She said she was coming down with a cold, he pleaded headache, but their excuses seemed capricious. I suspect they decided they had something better to do. I'm usually a peaceful person, but I felt like going over there, climbing up on their roof and pouring my pumpkin soup down their chimney. Would this have been a good way to indicate my displeasure?

—Now Stuck with Leftovers

Dear Now Stuck:

This is not the victimless crime some people think it is. These people are inconsiderate. You had every right to go over to their house, drag them back to your place and let them know what they missed by tying them to a chair and force-feeding them your black bean vegetable chili. My dinner guests never cancel because they know what's good for them: if they can't produce a doctor's note or a receipt for cold tablets, I call my lawyer and sue for breach of promise. (They always settle out of court.)

Futile Attractions

▼▼▼

"Do you have a sample Dear John letter that I could store in my computer?" asked one frustrated correspondent. "I'm tired of having to rack my brain every time I break up with a boyfriend." Having assumed that all couples love happily ever after (unless one tries to teach the other to drive a stick shift), I was appalled to find that love doesn't always conquer all. Reading so many letters from dissatisfied partners was almost enough to make me stop answering personal ads and, instead, buy a puppy.

True, most of the complaints were minor: a wife who told dialect jokes during sex; a man in despair because his CEO wife began love-making by advising him of his rights; a woman whose blind date, instead of being "cuddly," turned out to be violently plump (he was later charged with appearance in public under the influence of 14,500 Big Macs). But I took them seriously and hope my answers will assist those in search of domestic bliss.

Public Embarrassment

Dear Mr. Smith:

How do you feel about people who correct other people's pronunciation in public? When I happened to mispronounce "bourgeois" the other night at a gathering, my fiancé Alex corrected me in front of everybody. It was very demeaning. What should I do if this occurs again? I don't have time to look for a new source of strength.

—Mortified

Dear Mortified:

People who humiliate others in public must be dealt with severely, at least until they're in recovery. You can cut your fiancé down to size by gently (but wickedly) criticizing, in front of the others, his:

1. *Status in life*—"At least, Alex, I didn't get passed over for a promotion . . . again"*; or

2. *Attire*—"At least I don't go to parties with holes in my underwear"; or

3. *Manhood*—"At least I can have children."

✱ Alternate strategy: "So, my love, how come you're not earning more at your age?"

Double Agent

Dear Mr. Smith:

After dating a man for three months, I discovered that he's married. I'm furious at that sneak—he swore he got hair plugs just for me and I lost 10 pounds just for him. I want revenge.

—Sex Object

Dear Sex Object:

Now you know why he told you never to call him at home and was always on a "business trip" during holidays. Don't let him get away with it. Phone his wife and invite her to lunch (Dutch treat, of course). Explain in a nice way that you and her husband were having an affair and you want to:

1. Meet your competition.
2. Find out if his taste in a wife is as good as his taste in the Other Woman.
3. Compare his love letters.
4. Return his robe.
5. See how she feels about sharing.
6. Discuss your love child.

Someday My Prince Will Come

Dear Mr. Smith:

Why are blind dates so great on the phone and, supernatural luck notwithstanding, so disappointing in person? The last one described himself as a young Clint Eastwood (but turned out to look more like Clint's horse). Then, at the restaurant, all he did was whine about his ex-wife. I couldn't wait to get out of there. How do I deal with these people?

—Still a Romantic

Dear Romantic:

Either take an antacid and suffer through the evening or, from now on, demand a non-airbrushed photo in advance (if none is available, a face rubbing will do). You should also insist on notarized letters of recommendation from at least three former lovers. If you still have to bail out in the middle of a dinner date:

1. Ask for a doggie bag. (Why leave your half-eaten cheeseburger for him?)

2. Excuse yourself.

3. Go to the ladies' room and climb out the window. (If you're not athletic, go to the kitchen and ask the chef, "Is there a back way out of here?")

4. Take a taxi home.

5. If he calls, tell him you're going back with your ex.

———

ADDITIONAL BLIND DATE SURVIVAL TIP: Even if the fix-up was by a trusted aunt, exercise extreme caution. Over-the-phone descriptions can be treacherous.

A Man Who Says He's:	May Turn Out to Be:
A hopeless romantic	Unemployed
Zany and fun-loving	Chemically dependent
Comfortable with himself	Conceited
Ready to commit	An outpatient
Sensitive	Litigious
Emotionally mature	Dull
Very giving	Needy
Financially independent	On welfare
Very bright	On software
Warm and outgoing	A pouncer
Good at games	A compulsive gambler

Same-Knight Service

Dear Mr. Smith:

I'm extremely handsome, and I date about three times a week. Why is it that when a woman pays for dinner, she assumes, even if I skip dessert, that I'm going to have sex with her? Can I at least play hard to get? Respond soon, I'm very tired.

—Mr. Right

Dear Mr. Right:

I got several letters from men *and* women wondering how far they must go when their companion pays for dinner. It's kind of like a trade agreement: the more expensive the meal, the more the person who pays the check has the right to demand (unless, of course, the portions were small). Under $10 (including tip and garlic bread), for example, sexual favors needn't go beyond a peck on the cheek and, in the car, dividing the doggie bag evenly. Above $10, use the following chart:

Cost of Dinner	Person Who Pays May:
$11 to $15	Flirt, touch your knee under the table and help you on with your coat when you leave the restaurant.

Cost of Dinner	Person Who Pays May:
$16 to $21	Hug your waist as you walk to the car plus nuzzle your neck at the first stoplight.
$22 to $30	Rub against your chest, fondle you *above* the waist and ask you to help change the tire. Caution: Don't be fooled, this is a subtle form of foreplay.
$31 to $45	Expect you to come inside for liquid refreshment like a) a night-cap and b) a bubble bath.
$46 to $50	Carry you over the threshold.
Over $51	Remove the 25 throw pillows and stuffed animals from the bed, look at you meaningfully and ask if you practice safe sex.*

* You may decline if: 1) You have indigestion, 2) it's a school night or 3) you're not yet divorced.

Moochers

Dear Mr. Smith:

Save me from starvation! Whenever we're in an ice-cream shop, after ordering my usual three scoops, I ask my girlfriend who's always dieting, "Do you want anything?" "No," she replies. "Are you sure?" I ask. "Positive," she insists. But when we get in the car her first words are "Can I have a lick?" I love her, so I let her lick, but one pass with that earthmover tongue of hers leaves me with a nearly empty cone. Why doesn't she get her own?

—Deprived

Dear Deprived:

Because someone else's ice cream always contains fewer calories. Stop being so generous. The next time she asks for a lick, hand her some money, point toward the store entrance and ease her gently out of the car. My personal solution is more radical, however. The moment I get my four scoops of rum raisin and see my girlfriend's eyes light up, I hand her a raisin, then lick the ice cream all over and, for good measure, cough on it. This special "anti-sharing" technique disgusts even the most loving partner—it can also be used on hoagies and pizza slices.

You Haul It

Dear Mr. Smith:

Three weeks ago, without warning, my girlfriend left me for another man. Since then I've spent every evening at home, throwing darts at her photograph and surviving on a diet of Cheez Doodles and vodka. She just called and asked me to bring over the rest of her clothing, her books, the armchair we (sob) bought together and a jar of pickled herring she left on her side of the refrigerator. What should I do? (Please hurry, she's expecting me in half an hour.)

—In Pain

Dear In Pain:

I can't believe her nerve. First she dumps you, and now you're supposed to be her pack mule? Forget it! You'll feel much better if you take these simple steps:

1. Put the pickled herring on the radiator.
2. Go through the house and put tags on everything she owns.
3. Hold a garage sale. (Keep the armchair, however. If it contains painful memories, have it reupholstered.)
4. Use the proceeds to pay for a personal ad.
5. Mail her the pickled herring.

"It Drapes Well"

Dear Mr. Smith:

My wife is searching for the perfect cocktail dress. She drags me from store to store, telling me she'll "just be a minute," then makes me stand there guarding her purse while she tries on 500 dresses, each time emerging from the dressing room to ask, "How does this look?" Frankly, everything she tries on looks the same, and by the eighth outfit I start to tremble. Why can't she make up her mind?

—Rather Be Skiing

Dear Rather Be:

Because looking great in everything can be very perplexing. You could show your wife how it feels by making her wait when *you* go shopping, but no male of substance spends more than four minutes buying a suit. Offering your honest fashion opinion, however, may convince her to

SHOPPING TIP

Just outside their dressing rooms, better stores keep a "husband bench" where, while waiting for his wife to decide, an impatient husband is given the swimsuit issue of *Sports Illustrated*, a Miller Lite and two aspirins.

quickly say, "I can't find anything, let's get out of here," and cut your waiting time in half. The following comments have proven particularly effective:

For Any Dress	What to Say
With lots of patterns that the fitting room supervisor "just adores."	"Perfect for spilled drinks—the vermouth will never show."
That features the season's "newest colors" (lime/yellow).	"Gee, you look like a huge pineapple in heat."
You think is too revealing and may cause inferior men to drool.	"Entirely appropriate for stopping traffic or attending the funeral of a rock star."
That violates local fashion ordinances (makes her look like Madonna—Leonardo's).	"That dress looks the way I feel after my third Prozac."
That's knitted, skintight, shows off her figure and makes you feel like it's definitely time for a second honeymoon.	"We'll take it."

"Can We Watch One Thing?"

Dear Mr. Smith:

Every night my husband sits there clutching the TV remote control, clicking past program after program and making me crazy. Please help. I know I'm not the only woman whose husband is possessed. (I even confiscated the batteries, but he works for Duracell.)

—Feeling Remote

Dear Remote:

Use my system of reward and punishment. When he lets you watch a program all the way through:

▲ Bake his favorite cake.

▲ Stop answering the phone during sex (or at least make the conversation brief).

▲ Be kind when he anxiously points to his bald spot and asks, "Does it show?"

▲ Don't let him see your son's orthodontic bill.

THE PROPER THING

To make the marriage run smoothly, many pre-nuptial agreements now feature, along with references to money and property, a Non-Clicking codicil.

When he constantly clicks, get even:

▲ Be assertive and fight him for the clicker. If he's stronger, fight dirty—tickle him.

▲ Get into bed with cold feet and wearing rollers.

▲ Withhold sex (I'm sure you've already thought of that).

▲ When the "Shrink hemorrhoids without surgery" ad comes on, look at him knowingly.

▲ Go into labor during the playoffs.

———

CONFIDENTIAL TO "WHY, WHEN WE'RE IN BED, CAN'T HE HOLD SOMETHING ELSE IN HIS HAND?" IN CINCINNATI: The need to control the channel changer may be interpreted as an insecure male partner's need to exert power, dominate and feel in control, especially on Mother's Day. On the other hand, it simply may be his way of watching *Gunsmoke*, *The Waltons* and *Bullwinkle* reruns when they're on at the same time.

Chair Potato

Dear Mr. Smith:

My husband flops down in his easy chair the minute he gets home, then spends the rest of the evening reading Car *and* Driver *or watching television and stuffing himself with beer and Twinkies. There's never any communication, and I feel ignored. How can I get him to talk to me?*

—Lonely

Dear Lonely:

You could pique his interest by saying something provocative like "Dear, how much do you think it'll cost to replace the garage door? I didn't see it when I backed out." But why bother? Men like these are almost always beyond redemption. You'll have more fun starting over. If your husband's insurance exceeds $500,000:

1. Make sure you're the beneficiary.
2. Encourage him to smoke.
3. Encourage him to elevate his blood pressure by increasing his salt intake. Doctor's orders include:
   ▲ Pretzels
   ▲ Beer nuts
   ▲ Norwegian sardines
4. Remain inconsolable until the check clears.
5. Call me.

Viewer Discretion

▼▼▼

Silly me. I once thought that buying a ticket to a film or concert entitled me to an evening of pleasure. Unfortunately, our theaters have been taken over by a semicriminal class known to etiquette experts as barbarians: late arrivals who stumble around in front of you, blocking your view and making you miss half the picture (encourage them to sit faster with a pea-shooter), the 300-pound moviegoer who sits down next to you and hogs the entire armrest plus most of your seat (apply fat-sucking leeches until such person is reduced to a sample size), audience members who not only talk throughout the performance but, crime of crimes, make eating noises! Is it any wonder that I'm out on bail for turning a fire extinguisher on a popcorn muncher who, during my favorite movie (*Bambi*), kept smacking her lips? In civilized theaters, they remove the worst troublemakers with a licensed exterminator. Those deprived of this remedy may find the following section helpful.

Picnic in the Dark

Dear Mr. Smith:

I really resent it when I go to the movies and see a sign saying "Only food purchased in this theater may be taken to your seat." The popcorn costs more than my ticket, especially if I get butter (which usually tastes like Vaseline Intensive Care), and the candy and soda are outrageously overpriced. Dare I sneak in food, like an entire pizza, under my coat?

—On a Budget

Dear Thrifty:

Smuggling in a pizza is easy: put a slice or two in each pocket.* Before I go to a movie, I bake a meat loaf in the shape of an infant, diaper it and carry it to my seat. Between bites, to avoid detection, I rock it. (I recently, however, had to change my seat when the person next to me kept trying to tickle it under the chin.)

---

* Those with cellular phones will be happy to know that Domino's delivers as long as the movie theater you call from is showing a PG-rated film. Be sure to tell them your row and seat number.

CONFIDENTIAL TO PAM IN KANSAS CITY: Don't worry about eagle-eyed ushers. Eat your bucket of fried chicken undisturbed by concealing it under a lap robe.

"Pardon Me"

Dear Mr. Smith:

In a packed movie theater, how do I squeeze past the people who are already seated to reach an empty seat? Hardly anyone ever stands, and the real sadists barely move their legs aside. It's such a struggle.

—Theater Patron

Dear Patron:

Simply step on the feet of those who give you a hard time. (Apologize only to anyone wearing sandals or whose pedicure you ruin.) Or, as you pass by, take revenge by spilling a few drops of your soda on any audience members who seem particularly reluctant to move their legs. (Don't forget to say "Sorry.")

———

CONFIDENTIAL TO "HATE IT WHEN SOMEONE SITS NEXT TO ME" IN COMMACK MULTIPLEX: Another reply to "Is that seat taken?" is "Yes, it's my erogenous zone." No one wants to spend two hours in the dark sitting next to a mental case.

Snap, Crackle and Pop

Dear Mr. Smith:

What do I do when I'm at the movies and the person in front of me makes eating noises that drown out the sound track? If I lean forward and politely ask them to chew their popcorn or suck their Milk Duds less resonantly, I'm either ignored or glared out. It takes all the fun out of moviegoing.

—Sensitive

Dear Sensitive:

The real question is, why do they sell movie tickets to these accidents of evolution? When this happens, take out a rubber band and snap it against the nape of the offender's neck (two snaps are usually sufficient). If he screams, have an usher eject him for creating a disturbance. (*Caution:* If *he* summons an usher, wipe your fingerprints from the rubber band, stare straight ahead at the screen and admit nothing.)

———

CONFIDENTIAL TO "WHY CAN'T THE GUY IN FRONT OF ME SIP HIS PEPSI WITHOUT SLURPING?" IN CHICAGO: Quietly sew his shirt to the back of his seat. Look innocent when he springs up for more soda.

WHAT'S THAT NOISE?

▼▼▼

T o silence someone who constantly talks during a movie, take a deep breath and try a courteous "Shhhhhhhhhhh." If this fails, retaliate either by clamping your hand over the offender's eyes and blocking her view of the screen or bouncing several Chiclets off her head. A friendly but firm squeeze of the earlobe also may work.

If someone beside you is loudly tapping his foot or constantly whispering to his companion during a chamber music performance, follow the Haydn Quartet Rule: let him know he's behaving objectionably by gently but firmly tapping his knee either with a pencil or, if he's unresponsive, a ball-peen hammer. Incessant coughers, particularly those who cough during the pianissimos, are best disciplined by rolling up your program and tapping on their windpipe. (Two taps for "Please stop coughing, it's irritating"; three taps for "You need to see a doctor.")

Rock-a-Bye Baby

Dear Mr. Smith:

The other night at a Whitney Houston concert, a member of the audience nodded off and no one, not even the conductor, could poke him awake. He turned what should have been a sublime musical experience into an utter disappointment. Not only could I barely hear Whitney, but it was very painful—she was singing in the key of A-flat and he was snoring in G.

—Music Lover

Dear Music Lover:

Why don't these people do their sleeping where they're supposed to—at work? If you don't like confrontations, there are other ways to silence a public snorer:

1. Gently slide a plastic bag over his head (*caution:* may cause emphysema or you may need two bags if such person has a beehive hairdo) or, if you can still hear him,

2. Firmly grasp his nose and insert a Raisinet in each nostril.

PROTOCOL REMINDER

If your companion falls asleep at a concert, you are responsible for a) prodding him awake (unless it's *Das Rheingold* or Paul Anka) and b) interpreting his dream.

Dial "A" for Abuse

▼▼▼

T he problem with ordinary etiquette manuals: unsatisfactory information concerning how to get even with those who use the phone to intrude into our lives. How to deal with the emotional scars of rejection caused by friends who have Call Waiting and use it while we're on the phone with them? (Slam the phone down. When they call back, explain that you're eating baby back ribs and the receiver keeps slipping through your hands.) What to do about telemarketers who pester you with junk calls? ("They should be hunted down like dogs," wrote one correspondent.) On the subject of cellular phone abuse, several letters suggested establishing a special hell for people who use their phones on the sidewalk, oblivious to those around them and forcing anyone in their path to move aside or be trampled to pieces.

It Came from Outer Space

Dear Mr. Smith:

What do I do when people use their car phone to call me? Every five seconds we're cut off and I'm supposed to wait patiently while their car returns to Earth. If it's so urgent, let them pull over and use a pay phone.

—Still Holding

Dear Holding:

Statistics show that 89% of all calls from car phones are made by drivers stuck in traffic or a car wash and desperate for amusement. (Happily, many of them get rear-ended.) Their voice fades in and out while you sit there wondering when next you'll hear a human voice. Forget it. If the connection's bad, simply hang up. When they call back and say, "We must have been cut off," agree, tell them, "Next time, write," and then hang up again. Life is too short.

THE PROPER THING

So cellular phone owners know the torture they put you through, call them at home from a bowling alley phone on league night.

The Waiting Game

Dear Mr. Smith:

Are people who monopolize public pay phones protected by the Constitution? They know I'm waiting to make a call, yet they keep right on talking. And just when I think they're finishing and I get my hopes up, they get their second wind and continue for another 10 minutes!

—Still Trying to Call Home

Dear Still Trying:

And then, after yet another 15 minutes, they have the audacity to turn around and ask you for change of a dollar. I have no problem letting these people know I need the phone. After:

▲ *3 minutes*—Remind the caller that this isn't his living room.

▲ *4 minutes*—Get close and ask if you can say hello.

▲ *5 minutes*—Harass the caller either by correcting his grammar or turning up the volume on your boom box.

▲ *7 minutes*—Plug up the coin slots with gum.

▲ *10 minutes*—You're desperate and are therefore entitled to reach out and touch someone:

    1. Grab the caller's ankles.

    2. Pull.

    3. Leave no fingerprints.

6 THINGS TO DO WHEN YOU'RE PUT ON HOLD

▼▼▼

You've finally gotten through, but the other party has put you on hold. At this point, any red-blooded American would scream "Hold this, pal!" and instantly hang up. If, however, the call is important, pass the time pleasantly:

If You're:	Suggested Activity
Frustrated	Have a stiff drink.
Tired	Take a nap.
Hypochondriacal	Cock your head and listen to your heartbeat.
Waiting to hear if you got the job	Read the Bible and bite your fingernails.
Vengeful (and have just had the luncheon special at Taco Bell)	Breathe deeply and respond to the offender's "Sorry I kept you waiting" with a ringing belch.
Humiliated, angry and demeaned	Regain your self-respect: retaliate by placing the other person on hold, then call your therapist.

End of the Line

Dear Mr. Smith:

How do I end a phone call with a friend who keeps jabbering despite several hints that I want to get off? Each time I try to say goodbye, she slides into a new topic and goes on for another half-hour!

—Bent Ear

Dear Bent:

Don't you get it? People like your friend just like to hear themselves talk—you exist only to occasionally utter affirmative grunts. Next time she calls, try one of the following:

▲ Gently hang up in the middle of a sentence. She won't hear the click and will keep on chattering away, sometimes until the next day.

▲ Mention you have Call Waiting, put her on hold and go to Europe.

▲ If you don't value her friendship, mutter "I think I smell something burning, let me call you back." When you get off the phone, burn her phone number.

▲ If you value her friendship, put the phone down and go about your business. She'll never know.

NOTE: During the holiday season, I use "Pardon me, someone's coming down the chimney," and hang up.

ANSWERING MACHINES

▼▼▼

I receive many letters from people seeking the perfect answering-machine message. One correspondent asked whether "This is George's machine, speak" might be too curt. Another felt her message, "This is Barbara—if it isn't about money, sex or a new recipe, don't bother," wasn't warm enough. And one family's message, "We're not here, we've gone to Bermuda for two weeks, please don't rob us," was too candid.

Because I find no official precedent concerning the ideal message, I present my own as a role model:

Ring, ring.

"Hello, this is me. If you're calling to invite me to dinner, press '1.' If you want to know if I'm free to attend a great party on Saturday night, press '2.' If this is my mother, press '3.' If this is my mother calling again, press '33.' If you're a phone solicitor with a fabulous offer, press your receiver to the cradle. If this is a wrong number, press '4' and apologize. If you want to talk to me, please hold—I, or someone just like me, will be with you in a moment.

Civil Disobedience

▼▼▼

This section does not apply to the millions of dedicated civil servants whose devotion to duty (and their pension) makes our government run so efficiently. We are, rather, concerned here with a certain breed of petty official: the self-important bureaucrat who makes you wait while, between sips of coffee, he slowly processes your application (and becomes apoplectic if it's not filled out properly) or, between personal phone calls, actually picks up a piece of paper and, after shuffling it for several days, reads it (while moving his lips, of course). Also discussed are private-sector bureaucrats, claims processors and customer service representatives whose attitude problems make life wretched for those they're supposed to help. (*Note:* Medical researchers now suggest that many bureaucrats move so slowly owing to a previously undiagnosed condition known as "Red Tape Worm.")

The Customer Is Always ... a Nuisance

Dear Mr. Smith:

Last week at my bank when I needed assistance, I had to wait while the customer service rep finished what appeared to be a personal phone call (it had to be, her smile was sincere). Finally she looked up, annoyed, put her hand over the mouthpiece and uttered a perfunctory "May I help you?" as though to say, "How dare you, a lowly client, inconvenience me?" Alas, it's always afterwards that I think of something witty to say like "Yes, this is a stickup."

—Now Keeping My Money Under the Mattress

Dear Keeping:

Changing banks is not the solution—customer service reps are generic. Now when this happens to me, I wait five seconds (always give them time to finish their sentence) before snipping the phone wire. This a) ends the conversation and b) secures their undivided attention.

BANKS WITH A CONSCIENCE

▼▼▼

Along with recognizing a "Teller of the Month," certain banks are making amends by featuring a "Customer of the Month." In addition to free counseling, a plaque will be awarded to any individual who:

▲ Without fidgeting, waited on a line serviced by a teller unable to transact business until she finished describing last night's date to a co-worker.

▲ Did not participate in the ensuing melee when 22 irate customers attempting to do business on their lunch hour were told, "Our computers are down."

▲ Is still patiently waiting for the bank to explain a) how it lost a deposit and b) when it will make the money available.

▲ Kept the stiffest upper lip when refused a mortgage.

▲ Did not scream "DIDN'T YOU EVER HEAR OF A CHECKING ACCOUNT?" while waiting for the person in front to get six money orders from a lethargic teller.

▲ After eight attempts, still remained optimistic and finally found a working bank pen.

HAVING ENDURED the FDA, the FBI, the CIA, the IRS, OSHA and jury duty, I feel it's no wonder that Americans constantly need tranquilizers like bourbon and Snickers. How else to recover from an encounter with a government employee—especially a "lifer"?

One Mile per Hour

Dear Mr. Smith:

After standing on line for two miserable hours at my local motor vehicle bureau (it was hot, there was no air conditioning and I was out of Midol), I finally reached the window but was told by a surly employee that I was on the wrong line and to move out of the way. When I explained it was one of his co-workers who sent me there, he said, "Not my problem, lady" (at least, I think that's what he said; the English of some of these people is not like yours or mine), and turned his back on me. Suddenly, I knew why people buy assault rifles. I'd be grateful for advice should this happen again.

—Driving with an Expired Registration and Proud of It

THE PROPER THING

I never enter a motor vehicle office without bringing something big for moral support, like my Dodge van.

Dear Driver:

Taxpayer abuse by arrogant civil servants is universal. They:

▲ Take their breaks only when it's busy.

▲ Often speak in strange tongues.

▲ Move too slowly.

▲ Never look you in the eye.

▲ Gloat when the lines get really long.

The next time you're victimized at a government office:

1. Bribe the guard. (For $5, he won't interfere when you lose control. For $10, he'll help you.)

2. Shout "Your pension fund's in danger!" (Around civil servants this is like yelling "Fire!" in a crowded theater—they'll panic and work faster.)

3. Wail and rend your garments (a nice touch but don't ruin that expensive summer dress).

4. Hurl blank motor vehicle forms around the room.

5. Hurl blank motor vehicle employees around the room.

6. Calm down instantly when you get what you want. Smile and leave quietly.

MOTOR VEHICLE ETIQUETTE ADVISORY

Any driver whose photo ID makes him or her look either a) like a criminal or b) psychotic may have the offending picture retouched at state expense.

Health Care Reform

Dear Mr. Smith:

Despite innumerable phone calls and letters of complaint, my health insurance company refuses to pay my claim. I'm right, they're wrong. Can you help?
—Blue and Cross

Dear Blue:

The first rule is to avoid underlings and deal directly with the person in charge, like the president of the company. If he won't take your calls, adopt my exclusive "Hello, I'm trouble" system of justice:

1. *Crude but effective*—Find out where he lives and pay him a visit. Use one hand to ring his bell and the other to cradle that idling chain saw that will persuade him to do the right thing.*

2. *Peaceful but less effective*—Stand in front of the insurance company entrance holding a "Shame on You" placard. (Too passive, and what if it's raining?)

3. *Author's choice*—Contact him when he's most vulnerable. Find out where he plays golf. (They all play golf.) Each time he's about to putt, tap him gently on the shoulder and politely ask for your money . . . through a megaphone. (This will also work at the company picnic.)

---

*If he calls the police, explain you're a tree surgeon looking for work.

APPROPRIATE BEHAVIOR: FISTICUFFS

▼▼▼

I am alarmed by the number of letters containing the phrase "God, I wanted to punch him in the nose." Americans must be eating more red meat. Such behavior is justified only when:

▲ A condescending clerk insists, "Store credit only."
▲ You're having difficulty persuading an auto dealer to take back a lemon.
▲ A construction worker makes an obscene comment about your boyfriend's legs.
▲ You didn't get the raise you deserve.
▲ You're the victim of:
   a) a civil servant with an attitude
   b) a farmer who gave you wrong directions
   c) a fender bender
▲ A lenient judge didn't give the person who assaulted you enough time.
▲ In a restaurant, a strolling minstrel refuses to leave until he's finished his song.
▲ You see no other way to decisively settle an argument over politics or religion.
▲ You're unhappy with your personal trainer's performance.
▲ You can't get your lawyer on the phone.
▲ You tell your boyfriend that you're pregnant and he asks, "Is it yours?"

IRS Dearest

Dear Mr. Smith:

Last night I watched a television story on government waste. Today I got a letter from the IRS claiming I owe an additional $956 on last year's income tax. I'm outraged—I hardly used the federal government last year. Should I pay? I'd prefer to use the money to buy new power tools and contribute to a strong U.S. economy.

—Patriot

Dear Patriot:

Always remember: it's not what you earn, it's what you deduct. When I get a notice from the IRS informing me that I owe additional taxes, I simply check the appropriate line on the explanation form below and send it back. I encourage you to do the same.

Dear IRS:
I can't pay the additional taxes you claim I owe because:

___I've found a loophole.

___I've dropped out to find myself.

___I'm broke (Europe's gotten so expensive).

___I'm distracted by other events:
   ___My team lost the pennant.
   ___Discovered I was gay.
___I hoped you wouldn't notice.
___I need the money for other things (check only one):
   ___Food
   ___Medicine
   ___A campaign contribution
___I'm a tax-exempt organization:
   ___School
   ___Church
   ___Synagogue
   ___Mafia

——

CONFIDENTIAL TO "WHY ME?" IN NASHVILLE: Appeal to their sense of humor. On the appropriate line of your IRS audit notice, neatly write, "Come and get me."

Reach Out and Touch Someone

Dear Mr. Smith:

Phone solicitors are forever calling me just as I'm stepping into the shower or settling down with a drink after a hard day (how do they always know?). And they're persistent—even after I politely decline their offer to sell me waltz lessons or acreage in the Everglades, they just keep talking.

—Afraid to Answer My Phone

Dear Fearful:

Even the most determined telemarketer will instantly hang up if, in the middle of his spiel, you:

1. Begin singing "Stardust";

2. Quietly hand the receiver to your three-year-old daughter and tell her the nice man on the phone wants to hear all about her new dolly; or

3. Ask the caller if he's found God.

Travel Advisories

▼▼▼

Apparently, for travelers, the only thing worse than relying on the kindness of strangers is being at their mercy. "Have gun, will soon travel" is how one writer began her tear-stained fax, citing several examples of driver rudeness: an obscene gesture when she ridiculed the little animals adorning a driver's car window; a "fender bender" in which, instead of exchanging licenses, the perpetrator wanted to exchange photos (he had no license); and, worst of all, getting stuck behind a righteous citizen doing only 35 mph in a 35-mph zone. Equally victimized are airline passengers—those brave souls who, since deregulation, are not permitted to move about the cabin unless wearing their seat belt (a precaution, I assume, against whiplash). "I've been waiting here for hours," wrote one traveler, "hoping my luggage will soon turn up. Pardon the scrawl—it's difficult to write legibly when you're dizzy from watching an empty carousel go round and round."

Between always having to stop for red lights, constantly yielding the right-of-way, coping with dolts who hog the passing lane, annual inspections and not being allowed to park near a fire hydrant, it's a wonder we motorists have any fun at all.

The Open Road

Dear Mr. Smith:

I love to drive fast and my new Pontiac easily cruises at 100 mph, but those annoying road signs constantly remind me there are unreasonable speed limits. Fifty-five on the Interstate? 10 mph through a toll plaza? Get serious. My speedometer goes up to 120. Why waste all that performance? Don't you think all great drivers should be excused from observing unfair speed limits and given a special speeder's license? (Something official, like "This motorist has great reflexes and may go as fast as he or she wants.")

—Name Withheld

Dear Anonymous:

I agree. I can't tell you how many times I've arrived home with soggy tacos because I had to a) slow down to 50 mph through town, b) come to a nearly complete stop at several irksome stop signs and c) slow down to 60 on the exit ramp.

Here are the situations where exceeding the speed limit is justified:

1. You truly feel you are above the law.

2. You're a recovering speeder and you're late for a Speeders Anonymous meeting.

3. The scenery is unbearably ugly.

4. State trooper in pursuit, and you:
   a) Think you can outrun him; or
   b) Sincerely feel he has no reason to stop you; or
   c) Are a felon fleeing an outstanding warrant.

5. Eighteen-wheeler tailgating and you're trying to save your rear bumper.

6. You're bringing dinner home and do not wish to face the wrath of a family forced to eat cold Chinese food.

7. Curiosity: you want to see if speed bumps really work.

8. You've spent the last three hours trying to exit a cloverleaf and you're beginning to panic.

9. Hair not drying fast enough. (Convertibles only)

HIGHWAY DIPLOMACY

When pulled over for speeding, always compliment the officer on the superb tailoring of his uniform. You'll be let off with only a warning.

CONFIDENTIAL TO "FEEL GUILTY" IN MONTEREY: $2 is a stingy tip to a trooper who lets you off with just a warning when you explain you didn't realize you were doing 95 because you were keeping time to a Mariah Carey tape.

"One-Lane Traffic Ahead"

Dear Mr. Smith:

Whenever I'm in one of those six-mile traffic tie-ups caused by "Road construction next 10 miles," I wonder:
1. Why do our highway department geniuses pick the busiest time of the year to begin a project?
2. Why didn't they do it right in the first place?
—Engine Rapidly Overheating

Dear Overheating:

This is why I keep an emergency supply of Slim Jims in my glove compartment. Who knows when next I'll dine? In any traffic jam, you can eliminate that claustrophobic feeling by following these three steps:
1. Put your car in neutral.
2. Shut off the engine.
3. Close your eyes and take a nap. (In bumper-to-bumper traffic, your car will move forward courtesy of the vehicles behind you.)

NOTE: According to the EPA, "A motorist stuck in traffic who must heed the call of nature and is straining at his seat belt may put his vehicle in neutral and head for the nearest construction shack."

Contact Sports

Dear Mr. Smith:

Do you think rear-ending a slow-moving camper would make it move faster? On narrow country roads I always get stuck behind some lumbering Winnebago or Airstream, driven by a placid retiree or a guy with a bumper sticker saying "Don't come knockin' if the trailer's rockin'." They creep along, impossible to pass, the driver totally oblivious to the line of steaming motorists behind him.

—I Have Rights Too

Dear Empowered:

Why these people go unjailed is beyond me. A civilized society would allow them to sightsee only when there's minimal traffic, say at 3:26 A.M. I always urge these wrongdoers to move aside by playing the Good Samaritan— I blow my horn until the driver checks his side-view mirror, then I vigorously point downward, toward his left rear tire. He stops, I go. (If this doesn't work, I pass him on the right—isn't that what the shoulder of the road is for?)

ALTERNATE METHOD: During foliage season, one Vermont correspondent followed an offending Winnebago to a scenic overlook and made a citizen's arrest. (It held up in court.)

When Push Comes to Shove

Dear Mr. Smith:

How do you handle tailgating truckers? Four lanes of traffic—and I'm the one they pick on. Yesterday, in my rear-view mirror, I saw an 18-wheel monster only inches from my trunk, about to perform a crash test if I didn't get out of the way. Mr. Smith, you haven't been scared until you've been forced to do 75 mph in a Yugo with a shimmy. When I called the "How am I driving?" 800 number on the back of the truck, the driver's wife answered. She tried to sell me insurance.

—Ellen, Roads Scholar

Dear Ellen:

Truck drivers trying to make time are merciless. I regret that when I bought a new car I chose, as an option, a sunroof instead of a tail gun. The next time you're tailgated, slow down. When the trucker starts to pass you, speed up. Do this two or three times and watch in your rear-view mirror as he either jackknifes or pulls off the road to inspect the pills he's been popping.

Seat Belt

Dear Mr. Smith:

My husband, a compulsive back-seat driver, can't resist criticizing my driving: "Hey, slow down" . . . "Wow, darling, you almost hit that pole" . . . "Don't forget your turn signal, my love" . . . "Gee, sweetheart, what a sloppy turn." I happen to be a great driver. Would it be unwifely to make him ride in the trunk?*

—Road Amazon

Dear Amazon:

Better yet, pull up alongside an open manhole and make him get out. Fortunately, back-seat drivers *can* be rehabilitated. Stop at a scenic overlook and, while they're admiring the view, drive off. This will enable them to a) realize the error of their ways, b) perfect their hitchhiking skills and c) if they're over 80 years of age, become a historical marker.

> **ETIQUETTE ADVISORY**
>
> Neutralize a back-seat driver with a delicate stomach by stopping for lunch at any restaurant named "Mom's."

---

* Inviting your husband to drive might be a more satisfying option. Then you can say something neat like "What does it mean, dearest, when that little needle on the fuel gauge points to 'E'?"

HOTELS MUST BE improving. There were only 168 letters complaining about such minor annoyances as thin walls, overpriced room service, maids who enter the room first and then knock, and, of course, bellhops who have difficulty evaporating. Other correspondents, however, seemed to focus on one pet peeve, exemplified by the following letter.*

Weary Traveler

Dear Mr. Smith:

Must hotels have such early checkout times? No matter how tired I am, my only choice is to pay for another night or rush to check out and then finish sleeping off jet lag in the lobby. If they're so glad to see me, why do they eject me at 10 A.M.?

—Feeling Unwelcome

Dear Unwelcome:

I can't give you expert advice because I stay in hotels only when I need more towels. I do believe, however, that those establishments with early checkout times should be penalized. At $150 a night, why should you have to get up early for their convenience? My own system is simple: the earlier the checkout time, the more I borrow from the room to compensate for my pain and suffering.

---

* Failure to honor a reservation was another pet peeve. When this happens to one correspondent, a frequent business traveler, she grabs the desk clerk by the lapels, insists she qualifies for "homeless" status and demands to see a social worker.

If Checkout Time Is:	*I Take:*
Noon	A few washcloths and everything in the little gift basket (plus the basket itself if it's wicker)
11:30 A.M.	2 bath towels, 2 hand towels
11:00 A.M.	Blanket and pillow
10:30 A.M.	The coffee maker, one lamp and one picture
10:00 A.M.	The TV, Gideon Bible and one bathroom fixture

NOTE: If you're especially put out, feel free, when it's unattended, to help yourself to the contents of the maid's cart. (I possess an enviable collection of bath gel.)

A DMITTEDLY, I am phobic about flying, not only because of the Swiss steak but also because I'm convinced that the aircraft stays up only because I cling so tightly to the armrests. Flying used to be fun. But that was before anyone with the price of a ticket was allowed to board the plane. The privileges of democracy should go only so far.

The Wild Blue Yonder

Dear Mr. Smith:

When boarding an aircraft, I'm always anxious to reach my seat so I can a) begin reading Inflight *(can't get enough of those articles on "The New Tampa"), b) feel relieved that I'm not seated next to a mother with a colicky infant and c) pester the flight attendant for an extra pillow. How do I get the people in front of me to move faster?*

—Infrequent Flier

Dear Infrequent:

You can't. Instead, climb over the seats. People who dawdle when boarding an airliner are annoying, especially the ones who take an hour to find their seat (don't they know how to count?) or stow a rope-tied carton of grape-fruits in an overhead bin. All I want to do is get to my seat so I can start wondering whether or not the plane's going to crash. (*Tip:* If they're de-icing the wings with a scraper, get off.)

An Upper Berth?

Dear Mr. Smith:

On a flight to London, the child directly behind me kept kicking the seat, whining and hitting me over the head with his G.I. Joe. At first I just sat there, drinking Scotch, cursing my travel agent and wondering whether small children are considered carry-on luggage. Then, when I could stand it no longer, I turned around, smiled and asked the mother to please control her child. "What's he supposed to do for eight hours?" she snapped, and returned to her headphones. Because she was bigger and stronger, I had to endure this torment until we landed. What would you have done?

—Still Recovering

Dear Still:

Tilt my seat back till the kid was the same size as his G.I. Joe. On a plane, the air space around each passenger should be sacred. The next time a mother thinks her child deserves special consideration, why suffer? Either:

1. Let the flight attendants deal with this troubled youth (encourage the tyke to demand several rides on the beverage cart); or

2. Play "Hide and Go Seek" and lock him in the lavoratory; or

3. Place him on his meal tray and return both to the upright position.

151
▼

THE FOLLOWING LETTER confirms my belief that, in addition to bonus miles, airlines should dispense, free of charge, a tranquilizing agent called a "White Knuckle" and consisting of six parts cognac and one part maraschino cherry to any passenger whose fragile constitution prevents him or her from dealing with minor adversities such as:

▲ A near miss
▲ Someone else's child wanting to lie across your lap (the curse of three-abreast seating)
▲ Lost luggage
▲ Minimal legroom
▲ A bawling baby
▲ A nonstop talker in the adjoining seat
▲ Oxygen masks have dropped
▲ Flight attendant returned your meal tray to the upright position, alas with your potted beef still on it

Overfriendly Skies

Dear Mr. Smith:

How do I enjoy peace and quiet on an airplane when the passenger next to me keeps talking, refusing to accept that I wish to be left alone, even though I've shut my eyes . . . and my laptop on his hand?

—Lover of Solitude

Dear Lover:

In contrast to pilot error, this is known as "travel agent error"—you've been seated next to a bore. Fortunately, according to new FAA regulations, "a passenger may wrap in a blanket and stow in an overhead compartment any person who:

1. Exhibits snapshots of
    a. his or her family
    b. a dog, cat or hamster
2. Talks incessantly even though he can see that his seatmate is
    a. profoundly absorbed in
        i. a magazine
        ii. a sales report
        iii. the airsick bag
    b. feigning sleep
    c. actually asleep
3. Keeps pointing to your leftover lump of lasagna and asking, "Are you going to finish that?"
4. Gets up and climbs over his or her seatmate's legs five or more times in order to
    a. get a different magazine; or
    b. use the bathroom*
5. Takes up more than his or her share of the armrest because he or she is
    a. selfish, or
    b. 90 pounds overweight."

---

* The last time I flew, there was no pilot announcement about the laxative effect of their business-class muffins.

Some Restrictions Apply

Dear Mr. Smith:

On an airline flight, after I've finished eating, what's the correct way to let the cabin attendant know I want my meal tray removed instantly? The seats in economy are confining enough without having to sit there with that little shelf crushing my knees.

—Long Legs

Dear Legs:

Why busboys aren't included on meal flights I'll never know. Thanks to deregulation, however, there are several options. If you're:

1. *Tall*—Stow the tray in the overhead compartment.
2. *Short*—Place it in the aisle.
3. *Generous*—Hand it to the person seated next to you.
4. *Incontinent*—Leave it in the lavatory.

NOTE: Do not take your tray to the galley yourself, or the attendants will put you to work.

Sick and Tired

▼▼▼

A lthough hospital etiquette is still in its infancy, hundreds of letters from ex-patients made me realize that a hospital is no place for someone who's ill—every ounce of strength is needed to survive a) the cure and b) the well-wishers. Some correspondents complained of undergoing unnecessary procedures—one whose doctor instantly reached for a catheter when a simple nasal decongestant would have sufficed. Others mentioned the anonymity—complaining that their surgeon, obviously fearing a malpractice suit, actually wore a mask during the operation. I therefore felt obliged to relieve the suffering of people like Selma at Cedars of Lebanon, who wanted to know what to do about hospital gowns that "present a clear and present danger to one's dignity by flying open at the least provocation" (wear gaudy earrings to deflect attention), and "They're Stingy with Their Pain-killer" in Topeka (show them what stingy really means—don't pay your hospital bill).

Malpractice

Dear Mr. Smith:

Why do I spend more time in my doctor's waiting room than his plants do? If my appointment is for 3 P.M., for instance, I'm there on time. Then I wait . . . and wait . . . reading magazine after germ-laden magazine until finally, often an hour later, I get to see him. And no apologies! Why am I kept waiting so long?*

—Abused

Dear Abused:

Because a) you probably have one of those doctors who examine their patients too thoroughly and b) most doctors tend to overbook (they, too, have to put kids through college). Next time you see your doctor, go prepared. Bring:

▲ A laptop computer
▲ Snacks
▲ A change of clothing
▲ A deck of cards
▲ A cellular phone
▲ A few close friends
▲ Your lawyer

---

* Triage tip: While waiting, moan piteously. They'll take you first. (Will not work at the dermatologist.)

Intensive Care

Dear Mr. Smith:

I'm a hospital patient in a semiprivate room. When the wife of my roommate stopped by, the two of them drew the curtain and made what sounded like incredible love, grunting and moaning while I lay there frustrated and looking forward to a sponge bath from a homely nurse. If this happens again, I'll suffer a relapse.

—Temperature Rising

Dear Rising:

First, I find it incomprehensible that this man had the strength to make love on hospital food. Second, his wife should have brought a friend for you (they're usually found in the hospital gift shop). If this kind of thing happens again, summon the nurse, demand a sedative (gin works best for those recovering from a hernia operation) and put it on your roommate's bill.

CONFIDENTIAL TO "INVADING MY SEMIPRIVACY" IN HONOLULU: When noisy friends of the patient in the next bed won't quiet down, give them a reason to leave: pinch off his oxygen tube.

SHOULD YOU PAY YOUR HOSPITAL BILL?

▼▼▼

Many correspondents complained not only of skyrocketing hospital costs—$4 for an aspirin? $6.50 for fluffing a pillow?—but also that when they were finally discharged, they still didn't feel so hot.

Pay the bill only if you answer "true" to most of the following:

▲ I was greeted with a warm welcome. __true __false

▲ I was whisked to my room in a
wheelchair. __true __false

▲ There was a fireplace in my room. __true __false

▲ Complimentary newspaper brought
to my door. __true __false

▲ White wine always chilled. __true __false

▲ Mint placed on my pillow each night. __true __false

▲ I was able to eat the stewed prunes
without having to be held down by
orderlies. __true __false

▲ I was permitted to eat food brought in by friends:

  ▲ A smoked ham __true __false

  ▲ Kasha varnishkas __true __false

▲ I was never awakened at 3 A.M. to:

   ▲ Take a sleeping pill   ___true ___false

   ▲ Make a BM   ___true ___false

   ▲ Lift my feet so they could
     vacuum   ___true ___false

▲ I never had to use physical force to get rid of:

   ▲ A nurse waving a thermometer   ___true ___false

   ▲ A visitor   ___true ___false

   ▲ A hideous stuffed animal from
     the hospital gift shop   ___true ___false

   ▲ An orderly with an armor-
     piercing suppository   ___true ___false

▲ When I left, the hospital gave me:

   ▲ Flowers   ___true ___false

   ▲ My clothes back   ___true ___false

▲ I'm cured   ___true ___false

——

CONFIDENTIAL TO T.S. IN TOPEKA: It is unlawful for a hospital to refuse to discharge you because they need to keep their beds full.